DISPATCHES FROM THE DARK SIDE

On Torture and the Death of Justice

GARETH PEIRCE

VERSO

London • New York

In recognition of those who have come back into the light and have told what happened, and of those still in darkness.

First published by Verso 2010
© Gareth Peirce 2010
All rights reserved

The chapters in this book are based on articles that appeared in the
London Review of Books and are republished here, in a revised form, by
kind permission: Chapter 1, 14 May 2009; Chapter 2, 24 September 2009;
Chapter 3, 10 April 2008; Chapter 4, 13 May 2010 (under the title
'America's Non-Compliance').

3 5 7 9 10 8 6 4

Verso
UK: 6 Meard Street, London W1F 0EG
USA: 20 Jay Street, Suite 1010, Brooklyn, NY 11201
www.versobooks.com

Verso is the imprint of New Left Books

ISBN-13: 978-1-84467-619-4

British Library Cataloguing in Publication Data
A catalogue record for this book is available from the British Library

Library of Congress Cataloging-in-Publication Data
A catalog record for this book is available from the Library of Congress

Typeset in Fournier by MJ Gavan, Truro, Cornwall
Printed in Sweden by ScandBook AB

Contents

Preface

Each of these essays was written, at different times in the last two and a half years, as an urgent SOS—an attempt to set out the details of disturbing contemporary events, not all of which could easily be found in the commentaries of the daily news. Even less accessible in an instance such as this, where the facts suggest that the ship of state is sailing towards moral and political catastrophe, are the legal principles that might provide a life raft.

The last several years have found us in the midst of more such catastrophes than we could ever, in our worst nightmares, have dreamed of. We could never have envisaged that the history of the new century would encompass the destruction and distortion of fundamental Anglo-American legal and political constitutional principles in place since the seventeenth century. Habeas corpus has been abandoned for the outcasts of the new order in both the US and the UK, secret courts have been created to hear secret evidence, guilt has been inferred by association, torture and rendition nakedly justified (in the UK our government's lawyers continue to argue positively for the right to use the product of both) and vital international conventions consolidated in the aftermath of the Second World War—the Geneva Convention, the Refugee Convention, the Torture Convention—have been deliberately avoided or ignored.

It is the bitterest of ironies that John Lilburne, the most important originator of the rights we in this country and the United States claim and on which our respective constitutions, written and unwritten, were built, achieved this in large part as a consequence of his having been himself subjected to torture, to accusations based on secret evidence and heard by a secret court, to being shackled and held in extremes of isolation while exposed nevertheless to public humiliation and condemnation.

The worst excesses of the last nine years, which destroyed the certainties of those hard-won rights, should have sounded loud alarms, not least because of that precise historical parallel; one key in attempting to hang on to legal and moral concepts under attack is to remember their origin. Lilburne, an intractable young Puritan, with a strong sense of his rights as a freeborn Englishman, and a smattering of law, in 1637 was summoned before the Court of Star Chamber—a court comprising nothing more than a small committee of the Privy Council, without a jury, empowered to investigate. Lilburne had recently been in Holland and was charged, on the basis of information from an informant, with sending loosely defined 'fatuous and scandalous' religious books to England. His defence was straightforward: 'I am clear I have sent none.' Thereafter he refused to answer questions based on allegations kept secret from him as to his association with others suspected of involvement in the sending of the books; 'I think by the law of the land that I may stand upon my just defence, and that my accusers ought to be brought face to face to justify what they accuse me of.' For his refusal, he was fined £500, a fortune for an apprentice, and was lashed to a cart and whipped through the streets of London from Fleet to Westminster. He was locked in a pillory in an unbearable posture (in today's terminology a 'stress position'), but yet exhorted all who would listen to resist the tyranny of the bishops, repeating biblical texts to the crowd applicable to the wrongs done to him and to their rights. On being required to incriminate himself: 'No man should be compelled to be his own executioner.' He survived two and a half years in Fleet Prison, gagged and kept in solitary confinement, shackled and starving. The first act of the Long Parliament in November 1642 was to set him free, to abolish the Court of Star Chamber and to adopt a resolution that its sentence was 'illegal and against the liberty of the subject, and also bloody, cruel, wicked, barbarous and tyrannical.'

Lilburne's principled and public stance and the extraordinary political movement of which he was part, the Levellers, produced far more though than a brief reaction of abhorrence to the use of torture and arbitrary imprisonment. By the end of the seventeenth century, there had crystallised the foundation of the concepts upon which we draw now (and which we constantly choose to forget or ignore)—most importantly the concept of inalienable rights that pertain to the individual and not to the state. The Levellers insisted that the inalienable rights were possessed by the people and were conferred on them not by Parliament, but by God; no justification by the state could therefore ever justify their violation. For the preservation of these and the limitation of parliamentary power, the Levellers formulated a written constitution; never adopted in England, in the new world it became a political reality. In both countries, due process—the legal concept that gives effect to the idea of fairness—was born from these ideas.

Once evidence of any country's willingness to resort to torture is exposed, reactions of decency and humanity can be invoked without the necessity of legal explanation. Less likely is any instinctive reaction to evidence of the destruction of concepts of procedural fairness. Yet, in the imprecision and breadth of accusations, leading in turn to the banning of books and the criminalisation of ideas and religious thought, and in the wrong committed by secret courts hearing secret evidence, the lessons of John Lilburne and Star Chamber have been in the last nine years deliberately abandoned and sustained battles have still to be fought to reclaim the majority.

The shocking, reckless and ruthless disregard of all of these concepts seen in recent years is neither new nor unique to this country or to the US. The history of regions other than our own shows how fragile are the laws and their applications that we assume protect us when faced with a government determined to follow a contrary path. Repeatedly, historically, even nations which have recently emerged from the fires of hell remember the experience as it relates to themselves, but yet consign others to the same fate. Fewer than ten years after the end of World War Two, and only eight years from the UN Declaration of Human Rights, the first reports of the use of torture by the French against Algerians fighting their war of independence began to emerge, with justifications that today appear very familiar. (The first official reports in 1955 admitted some violence had been done to prisoners suspected of being connected to the FLN, but that this was 'not quite torture'; 'The water and the electricity methods, provided they are properly used, are said to produce a shock which is more psychological than physical and therefore do not constitute excessive cruelty.') Sartre articulated the shock of realizing that torture had reappeared and was being justified so soon after it had been categorised as an aberration found only among psychotic and degenerate governments willing to violate all universally understood and recognized principles of justice:

> In 1943 in the Rue Lauriston, Frenchmen were screaming in agony and pain; all France could hear them. In those days the outcome of the war was uncertain and we did not want to think about the future. Only one thing seemed impossible in any circumstances: that one day men should be made to scream by those acting in our name.

The illustration on the cover is of Shafiq Rasul, a young Englishman from Tipton in the West Midlands, who within hours of returning from unlawful captivity in Guantánamo Bay understood the need to put on record the reality of imprisonment there. For the next month, with Asif Iqbal and Ruhal Ahmed, he struggled to prepare a report, illustrated by sketches in the absence of any photographs, of what had been done to them. Soon thereafter, the legal challenge his family had initiated when he was first reported to be in Guantánamo (*Rasul v. Bush*) was decided by the US Supreme Court in favour of Shafiq Rasul. What argument was won? That the prisoners in Guantánamo Bay should have access to legal remedies and to lawyers who could, most importantly of all, for the first time go in and, bit by bit, bring out reports, not just of the physical and mental horrors inflicted by or on behalf of Americans, but of the complicity of this country (at every level) in their unlawful captivity. We were never meant to know any of this. The still unanswered question of burning relevance, however, remains: once we know, what do we then do?

July 2010
Gareth Peirce

1

'Make sure you say that you were treated properly'

Eight years ago now, in January 2002, came the first shocking images of human beings in rows in aircraft, hooded and shackled for transportation across the Atlantic, much as other human beings had been carried in slave ships four hundred years earlier. The captor's humiliation of these anonymous beings—unloaded at Guantánamo Bay, crouched in open cages in orange jump-suits—was deliberately displayed. For the watching world no knowledge of international humanitarian conventions was needed to understand that what it was seeing was unlawful, since what is in fact the law precisely mirrors instinctive moral revulsion. The definitions of crimes against humanity, and war crimes, are not complex: 'Grave breaches of the Geneva Conventions of 12 August 1949', including 'torture or inhuman treatment'; 'wilfully causing great suffering, or serious injury to body or health'; 'wil-fully depriving a prisoner of war or other protected person of the rights of fair and regular trial; unlawful deportation or transfer or unlawful confinement.' What the world could instantly see for itself in those images was that this was the trafficking of human beings. It was not a manifestation of the Geneva Conventions at work; it was neither deportation nor extradition: far worse, it was transportation from a world and to a world outside the reach of the law, and intended to remain so. In those two worlds, crimes against humanity were to be perpetrated, but they, unlike the images of transportation, were intended to remain for ever secret. That they have not has come about largely through chance.

Moments of major moral and political importance are often triggered accidentally, and how they are resolved depends entirely on whether public attention can be sustained. We are presented with such a moment now. The possibility has come about in large part through the case of Binyam Mohamed, where in the High Court a battle continued for more than two years to discover even part of the true relationship between British intelligence and the Americans and Moroccans, who for eighteen months slashed the most intimate parts of his body with razors, burned him with boiling liquids, stretched his limbs causing unimaginable agony, and bombarded him with ferocious sound. At the same time, dedicated journalists have accumulated evidence—too much to be swept aside—of men tortured just as horrifically by officials in Pakistan, who exchanged information with their British counterparts. Combined, these two sets of so far partial revelations have provided Britain with a moment of acute discomfort, sufficient to provoke the prime minister to announce the need for new guidelines for interrogations conducted by the intelligence services. This moment of official embarrassment should, however, make us in Britain feel the greatest disquiet. We inhabit the most secretive of democracies, which has developed the most comprehensive of structures for hiding its misdeeds, shielding them always from view behind the curtain of 'national security'. From here on in we should be aware of the game of hide and seek in which the government hopes to ensure that we should never have a complete understanding of its true culpability.

The opportunity for concealing the extent of our country's collusion with those who have carried out the actual torture is increased by three factors: first, the nature of most of the techniques used ('stealth methods', so called); second, the choking powers of secrecy available to our government; and third, the haphazard way in which acutely inadequate information about these matters emerges, when it emerges at all, hampering our ability to ask the most basic of questions.

We are now in the endgame of a cycle that started in late 2001. In the US the Obama administration, pushed by Freedom of Information Act inquiries, has released much of the most obscene evidence of what the previous administration consciously and specifically permitted. Storm clouds of retribution may be gathering around those who have perpetrated crimes against humanity. But what needs to concern us in Britain is this: while those first images put out by the US military in January 2002 gave a glimpse of what the US was doing, and prompted in that country a seven-year public debate about the Bush/Cheney/Rumsfeld redefinition of torture and abusive practices, here we remain almost completely in the dark about the part played by our intelligence services, and in turn by our Foreign Office and our Home Office and our ministers. There are no dramatic images to jolt us into comprehension and there is no release whatsoever of the information that US citizens claim it as their right to know. Yet we were there at those sites of unlawful confinement; in many cases it was we who told the Americans where to locate British nationals and British residents for rendition; it was we who provided information that could be and was used in conditions of torture; and it is we who have received the product.

Torture is the deliberate infliction of pain by a state on captive persons. It is prohibited and so is the use of its product. The UN Convention Against Torture and Other Cruel, Inhuman or Degrading Treatment or Punishment emphasises that there are no exceptional circumstances at all justifying its use, whether state of war or threat of war or any other public emergency; none of these may be invoked as a justification. Orders from superiors are explicitly excluded as a defence, and moreover the Convention requires that wherever the torture occurred and whatever the nationality of the torturer or victim, parties must prosecute or extradite perpetrators to a country that is willing to prosecute them.

Whatever its position in respect of denying knowledge of the Moroccans' treatment of Binyam Mohamed or of the most extravagant atrocities in Pakistan, the UK will undoubtedly try to remove itself several steps further from any knowledge of what has been done in secret sites by the US. But the tortures of which it is impossible that UK officials were not aware, those which have across the board characterised US treatment of prisoners in Afghanistan and Guantánamo, belong to families of torture descended from Western European and particularly British military punishments. Those who have categorised these things place them in the 'lesser' tradition of stress torture; not because they are less painful, but because they leave less of a visible mark. Prolonged restraint in almost any position will produce agonising muscle pain. To be compelled to stand without movement for twenty-four hours causes ankles and feet to swell to twice their size. After that, to move is to be in extreme pain; large blisters develop, the heart rate increases, many people faint, and eventually the kidneys shut down. Prisoners suspended by the wrists have their feet touching the ground so that the weight is shared between wrists and feet, but this serves only to increase the time prisoners may be suspended, extends the pain and delays the emergence of permanent injury. That matters in what is known as stealth torture. It was in Mandate Palestine that British soldiers and police after 1938 subjected prisoners to suspension, forced standing, forced sitting and choking with water, and exposure to extremes of heat and cold. These tortures left no visible trace and could safely be denied. Today the interrogation style of the Israeli GSS—called 'shabeh' by its victims—continues to draw on the same techniques and on those used by the British in Northern Ireland. They include sleep deprivation, positional tortures, exhaustion exercises, exposure to extremes of temperature, the use of noise, and 'chair' torture. It is from these and their predecessors that the Americans have drawn for the last seven years.

In 1997, Nigel Rodley, then the UN special rapporteur on torture, very specifically reaffirmed his condemnation of these methods as torture:

> Each of these measures on its own may not provoke severe pain or suffering. Together—and they are frequently used in combination—they may be expected to induce precisely such pain or suffering especially if applied on a protracted basis of, say, several hours. In fact, they are sometimes apparently applied for days or even weeks on end. Under those circumstances, they can only be described as torture.

Since these have been the techniques most repeatedly deployed since 2001 on US sites where we know British personnel have been present, we need to establish that our government acknowledges that they are indeed torture. All have been described in detail by those British detainees who have returned from Guantánamo, and yet their testimony has been disregarded by those in government departments whose job it is to know. We had no difficulty understanding that these methods were torture when our enemies used them: during the Second World War we had no difficulty comprehending that the ordeal of British POWs forced by the Japanese to stand for days in a tin hut in the brutal heat was a war crime; and we recognised that in Stalin's gulags standing and sitting while being deprived of sleep was torture too. And yet Britain still, in 2009, appears to have the greatest difficulty in admitting that what was done routinely in Afghanistan and at Guantánamo Bay was torture, and even greater difficulty in admitting that we knew all along that it was happening. By the summer of 2002, White House lawyers were listing techniques that they considered would not constitute torture under the Federal Torture Act, among them forced standing, hooding, deprivation of food and drink, the 'frog crouch', the Israeli shabeh, and extreme noise.

And yet we of all nations must have immediately recognised these techniques for what they are and must have known that they were prohibited, since we were disgraced for employing them by the European Court less than thirty years ago. In August 1971 British soldiers arrested 342 men in Northern Ireland claiming that they were IRA suspects. To force their confessions, twelve of them were taken to a secret site and subjected to the now notorious five techniques (forced standing, hooding, sleep deprivation, starvation and thirst, and white noise). Most of the men later reported experiencing auditory hallucinations; the interrogators referred to the room used for noise as the 'music box', and were aware that the detainees were exhibiting distorted thought processes. The Republic of Ireland took the UK to court in Strasbourg for their use of these methods and Britain gave an unconditional promise never to use them again. And yet since November 2001, knowing that these techniques were being adopted (and even enhanced) in Britain's joint operations with the US, our ministers, ministries and intelligence personnel have behaved as if a blind eye could lawfully be turned while at the same time availing themselves of the same sites and sharing the product of those illegal methods.

In official advice, sent in January 2002 to MI6 personnel in Afghanistan concerning their own interrogations of detainees held by the US, it was stated: 'You have commented on their treatment. It appears from your description that they may not be being treated in accordance with the appropriate standards. Given that they are not within our custody or control, the law does not require you to intervene to prevent this.' This advice was then hedged with homilies: British personnel 'cannot be party to such ill treatment' and should not condone it. Yet as any first-year law student knows, encouragement by any number of indicators can expose the bystander to as much criminal liability as the main perpetrator.

The Intelligence and Security Committee, quoting this advice in the first of its two inquiries into the role of the intelligence services in 'the handling of detainees' since 2001, nevertheless blacked out in its report what the 'ill treatment' consisted of. Yet this is the only body in existence with the power to inquire into and give us answers about the intelligence services. Staggeringly, not only do we therefore still know nothing of what the intelligence services actually witnessed in Afghanistan, but in each of the committee's inquiries into their involvement or otherwise in torture, the government's witnesses and the committee in turn appeared to miss entirely the wider legal and moral point.

Instead, they focused on individual errors of judgment, even though members of the intelligence services were present during unlawful transfer and confinement: that is, in situations comprehensively meeting the definition of internationally prohibited crimes against humanity.

Equally disturbingly later in 2002, some months after MI6 sent its advice, the recently arrived British ambassador to Uzbekistan inquired urgently of the Foreign Office what its legal justification was for receiving information from Islamic dissidents who had been boiled alive to extract it. Craig Murray records his astonishment on being recalled to London to be told that Foreign Secretary Jack Straw and Sir Richard Dearlove, the head of MI6, had decided that in the 'War on Terror' we should, as a matter of policy, use intelligence obtained through torture by foreign intelligence services. A follow-up memo from a Foreign Office legal adviser in March 2003 explained that it was not an offence to do so. How sound was this advice legally? Morally, there is no question. But what of the encouragement to torture resulting from our enthusiastic receipt of information?

There have been no resignations over any of this. The government on whose watch it has occurred may be vulnerable for other reasons, but at present it seems not for possible complicity in grave crimes. From where does it derive its confidence? Control of information is a powerful tool: the answer must undoubtedly lie in the extent to which the secret state believes it has consolidated and can control any mechanism that might allow discovery and challenge. It can rely on its citizens never knowing properly, or often not know at all.

Since the end of the Cold War, there has been unprecedented worldwide monitoring of man's propensity to torture, and yet far from abating, its use has burgeoned. The explanation of how this has come about is to be found in the dual strategies upon which the monitoring of torture depends; the first, exposing it to public condemnation through the recording and publication of unchallengeable research, and the second, where torture has been conducted, holding state agents responsible. The first has spurred torturers to adopt the 'lesser' techniques, harder to detect and document. The second has encouraged governments to seek acceptance of their methods from a public quick to condemn those considered to be soft on terrorism. In this country, in fact, the government hardly needs such acceptance, since here the additional and crucial factor is that the public is unlikely to be given sufficient information to trigger revulsion.

Whether we will in this country ever know the full extent of British participation in criminal acts of the utmost seriousness should be a burning issue. We should not take it for granted that court cases or a judicial inquiry will tell us what we need to know about the complicity of our government in crimes against humanity. The Baha Mousa inquiry into the activities of the British military in Iraq will not touch on the interaction of the British state with the US or the intelligence services, or with any torturing foreign state. Instead, the government will claim, as it does with ever greater frequency, that any issue relating to the intelligence services, or to the conduct of diplomatic relationships, should be confined entirely to special courts, or the evidence heard in large part in secret. The use of these procedures expands daily.

This is not the way that the most basic principles of democratic responsibility and due process should be exercised even in the most mundane of circumstances; even less so when the issues are of such moral seriousness and public importance. To understand how we have come to this pass, graver than that in any other comparable democracy, we need first to understand how secrecy has come to be justified by successive governments, and to understand how the use of obfuscatory language has taken the place of informed democratic debate.

We still live, in the twenty-first century, in a world whose political configuration is that of the nation state. For those exercising political power, the issue of a nation's security, its 'national security', is of immense importance. The state is invariably referred to as a source of the security necessary for protection against threats from others, or from internal violence, and this idea is shared, by and large, by its population. There may be disagreement about the existence or gravity of any alleged threat and the appropriate response to it, but the concept of the state as the protector and guarantor of security is seldom doubted. 'Security' is such a dramatic yet ill-defined concept that those in power are able to muzzle criticism and prevent debate by invoking it and by claiming to possess vital knowledge (which cannot, of course, be safely revealed) to support their policies or their actions. Those in power draw on traditions of deference and non-partisanship when it comes to national security, allowing governments to avoid provision of any reasoned justification when it is said to be at stake. There is therefore a dangerous circularity to the entire process. Deference is fed in part by ignorance, and ignorance is fed in turn by claims that secrecy is essential. The public receives only the barest of justifications, to be taken on trust, while the government machine ignores or short-circuits normal democratic processes.

The language used is itself a critical contributing factor. After the Second World War the US was the first nation to transform traditional terminology, moving from 'defense' to 'national security' as the guiding ethos of its foreign policy, a conscious choice of words intended to reflect the expansion of the US's desired role in world affairs, conflating a myriad different political, economic and military factors so that developments elsewhere in the world could automatically be construed as having a direct impact on the US's vital national interests. Every development the world over came to be perceived as potentially crucial, an unfavourable turn of events anywhere endangering the United States. American foreign policy goals came to be translated into issues of national survival, and the potential threats without limit.

A similar mindset came to be consolidated in Britain by a quite separate route. In the wake of the Second World War the members of the Council of Europe, then only a few nations, committed themselves to a treaty, the European Convention on Human Rights, which provided for individual petition and was designed to give teeth to the enforcement of those rights. Several rights had caveats attached to them in case of exceptional circumstances, one of which was 'national security'. This was a new term in Europe: the phrase used by Britain and France until then had been 'defence of the realm', which reflected the most extreme threat a nation might face—that is, war. The British lawyers responsible for drafting the European Convention had been affected, it would seem, by the new postwar US conception, and adopted it wholesale.

While it may be that we are too far down the road to reclaim the old terminology, we should nevertheless insist on confining the application of the term 'national security' to core principles, including the protection of democracies from foreign invasion or manipulation, i.e. the ability to defend nation-states against military attack. In the minds of many people, however, and particularly in abbreviated media discussion, a further conceptual leap has taken place, so that secrecy and national security have now come to be seen as synonymous.

We allowed this state of affairs to come about through sheer neglect. Britain was the last of the parliamentary democracies to put any of its security and intelligence agencies on a statutory footing, and even into the 1990s it obstinately maintained the extraordinary fiction that MI6 did not exist. When belatedly, in the mid-1990s, there was talk of bringing the three intelligence services, MI5, MI6 and GCHQ, into a structure of accountability, a limited degree of oversight was given to a Parliamentary Committee on Intelligence and Security. But such parliamentary debates as there were failed to address fundamental questions, in particular those of limitation: what kinds of conduct do we as a society wish to declare off-limits? There has never been any sign in this country that any government has understood the need to talk through the issues involved, let alone promote public debate. So far as standards or controls were concerned, it was argued at the time that these were inappropriate and unnecessary because the organisations were controlled by their parent departments in ministries and required approval by ministers for all contentious actions.

Although the resulting legislation was in a narrow legal sense intended to bring the intelligence services onto a statutory footing, the wider political dimension was that an opportunity was there—it was missed—for the law to provide a primary statement about how our society believed its international dealings in particular ought to be conducted.

The Parliamentary Committee itself, a very British affair composed of high-ranking members of the House of Commons and House of Lords who had been security cleared, was left without any coherent brief in relation to oversight and was explicitly banned from receiving information about particular operations. Its primary concerns related to finance and administration. Yet, in the face of what in any questioning society might threaten the collapse of a government, it is this committee, operating as it does on such a narrow remit within an ethos of secrecy, that has been tasked by the prime minister with reordering the ethical basis of the intelligence agencies, seemingly without any comprehension on his part of the scale of what is required. This, it seems, is intended to act as our national catharsis. Yet we are unlikely to find out any meaningful detail. It is an irony that the death of Baha Mousa, killed by the military in a war zone, was nevertheless considered in open court martial.

If we look carefully there is sufficient evidence that British foreign policy, and indeed its domestic policy, have for many years been conducted in a way that is in violation not only of our own law and of international law, but which, far worse, has led us to be complicit in torture and in the commission of internationally prohibited crimes against humanity. No more serious circumstance could come to pass. At present, instances are explained away—when they briefly, accidentally come into view —as mere blips. An individual officer, for example, may not have been properly briefed on the prohibited techniques being used by the Americans. But taken overall the excuses produced one by one begin to wear thin. The High Court, constrained as to detail by the government's claim that secrecy is needed in the interests of national security (to enable the free flow of information with our US ally), nevertheless commented that the role of the UK in Binyam Mohamed's torture went 'far beyond that of a bystander' and triggered a criminal investigation into complicity on the part of at least one officer from MI5 in Mohamed's torture. That the excuses are produced individually, and are intended to remain separate, is part of their efficacy. Who is putting the excuses together? Whose task is it to investigate? What is the evidence that we ourselves can piece together? Whose job is it to find the evidence, in a situation where it has become too embarrassing and uncomfortable not to be seen to be looking for it?

The fact of the matter is that when it comes to the most important of crimes, such as the ones discussed here, individual citizens in any country can initiate a prosecution provided they assemble evidence sufficient to obtain a summons. (Even now, a number of former senior military or political figures enter the UK and other countries with considerable caution.) If a more formal reckoning is to be made, access to evidence is just as fundamental.

The clear intention of the British government is to bury any opportunity for public discussion before it starts. It is all the more critical, therefore, that we demand that it acknowledges the moral as well as the factual and legal dilemmas in which we are hopelessly entangled. As good a starting-point as any is to insist that it accept the severe condemnations issued by institutions and organisations that we are committed by international treaty to respect—and in the case of the European Court of Human Rights to obey—and in whose reports the United Kingdom has been singled out for criticism of unusual severity.

Carefully and painstakingly for a number of years since 9/11, a number of significant international organisations have unpicked what the nations of the world have done in response, and yet there is no sign that the resultant documents are even read by our government.

The relevant special rapporteur reporting to the UN General Assembly in February 2009 on this issue (the promotion and protection of human rights and freedoms while countering terrorism) selected the UK for special mention, for having interviewed detainees held incommunicado by the Pakistani Inter-Services Intelligence or ISI (held in so-called safe houses and tortured) and for its active participation, through the sending of interrogators or questions or intelligence personnel to places of detention where the rights of detainees were being flagrantly violated. The special rapporteur considered that such behaviour 'can be reasonably understood as implicitly condoning such practices', and that 'the continuous engagement of foreign officials in some instances constituted a form of encouragement or even support.' The special rapporteur further considered that 'the active or passive participation by states in the interrogation of persons held by another state constitutes an internationally wrongful act if the state knew or ought to have known that the person was facing a real risk of torture or other prohibited treatment, including arbitrary detention.' This, of course, is what has been staring us in the face in Afghanistan and Guantánamo Bay.

We need to take note of these views in order to appreciate how out of step Britain is with the true moral and legal universe. It is impossible forever to contrive excuses when the objective assessment of rendition, for instance, is this: 'While this system was devised and put in place by the United States, it was only possible through collaboration from many other states.' We should remember that the special rapporteur is only one of a number of

UN and EU bodies to have shone a light on these practices and all include Britain as a primary player in inter-state complicity.

The special rapporteur emphasises the position in law as well as morality. States 'are responsible where they knowingly engage in, render aid to or assist in the commission of internationally wrongful acts, including violations of human rights. Accordingly, grave human rights violations by states ... should therefore place serious constraints on policies of co-operation by states, including by their intelligence agencies, with states that are known to violate human rights.' This clearest possible statement of the overriding necessity of observing human rights cannot coexist with the claim, constantly made, that our country's paramount commitment must be the sharing of information with regimes, however heinous they may be, in the name of 'suppression of terrorism'.

We know that UK intelligence personnel conducted or witnessed more than two thousand interviews in Afghanistan, Guantánamo and Iraq. It is entirely inconceivable that any proper legal advice or any responsible government official could have considered for a moment that, for example, detention in the circumstances that pertained to Kandahar or Bagram in Afghanistan, or at Guantánamo Bay, was anything other than arbitrary detention outside of the law, and that these conditions were designed to break the human spirit for the purpose of obtaining information.

How do such stinging condemnations by international bodies play out in the current day-to-day behaviour of Britain and its foreign relations? The answer is extraordinary: there is no coherent reaction, and the government remains unmoved by criticism. Take Syria, for instance, the country which was most comprehensively exposed as a state that practised torture with the connivance of the Americans, when the Canadian Maher Arar was finally released from the twelve months of torture that followed his rendition. The Canadian government conducted a soul-searching public inquiry and paid Arar millions of dollars in compensation in acceptance of its contributory role. In April 2009, in contrast, Bill Rammell, our Foreign Office minister with responsibility for the sharing of information about terrorism, visited Damascus despite the disappearance in Syria weeks before of two British citizens. The Foreign Office, attempting to reassure the families that efforts were being made to find them, said that they had emphasised to the Syrians that 'this is a big issue at home at the moment'.

To understand that each episode is regarded by the government as a matter of importance 'at the moment'—i.e. finite and distinct that will no doubt blow over—it is vital to appreciate that in the handful of cases about which we know something, such knowledge has come to light only through an extraordinarily slow-moving series of events in which the veils of secrecy have been partially lifted only by accident, and that at every stage our government has fought against there being any revelation at all. This was true in the case of Binyam Mohamed, seized in the wholly lawless world of human ransacking in Pakistan in early 2002, and delivered by the Americans to Morocco. His brutal interrogation was based in large part on material provided by British intelligence, in files sent from the United Kingdom. He was considered by the authorities in America, Britain, Morocco and Pakistan to be a piece of flotsam whose disappearance would never be noticed and about whose fate state secrecy in whichever country involved would be forever guaranteed, being consolidated ultimately in his shipment to Guantánamo, outside, it was believed, the reach of the law. That these assumptions were ever contradicted came about as the result of a series of separate events, step by step, each step entirely a matter of chance.

First came the early images of Guantánamo, whereby the short-sighted triumphalism of the Americans, wanting to broadcast their images of dehumanised captives, failed to anticipate the efficacy of those images to provoke an entirely different reaction.

In Tipton in the West Midlands in January 2002, a young British man called Habib Rasul saw on television those first images of orange-suited detainees in Guantánamo just as a reporter from the Sunday newspaper of MI5's choice arrived at his door to inform him that his brother Shafiq was being held there. So much for state secrecy. Habib, a student whose political science project had been the lawless West Midlands Serious Crime Squad in the 1970s and its success in achieving the wrongful conviction of scores of innocent men, determined that there must be a legal inroad. He found lawyers in the UK, who in turn could now provide what lawyers in the US were desperately seeking: a named litigant to challenge the assertion that habeas corpus could not apply to those held at Guantánamo. Two and a half years later the US Supreme Court determined in *Rasul v. Bush* that the orange jumpsuited men, intended to remain for ever outside the reach of the law in Guantánamo Bay, could see security-cleared American lawyers.

And so it was that in 2005 Binyam Mohamed could first give an outside visitor an account of his rendition and torture in 2002, and of the complicity of the British at every stage; and so it was that, in 2009, on the basis of this account, his lawyers in the UK could construct a legal proposition of significance: if the British intelligence services knew that he had been tortured, and that the torture had produced a confession which was being used to underpin a prosecution in the mockery of a court that called itself the Military Commission in Guantánamo Bay, then British intelligence must have evidence that would assist his release. Thereafter a sorry saga of misleading evidence by ministers, lost files, overlooked memoranda and forgotten vital facts unfolded in the UK courts. Mohamed, mercifully, has meanwhile been returned from Guantánamo. But the principle that he, a foreign national, could return to the UK, to the country in which he had lived, had been contested tooth and nail by the British government.

It was in fact a further twist of fate that finally forced the government to change its position on the issue of the return of UK residents from Guantánamo. As is now well known, two law-abiding, innocent non-nationals, both permanent residents of Britain, travelled to Gambia in November 2002 to set up a business there. One of their party, a British citizen, returned. Those without British nationality were seized by the Americans, taken to Afghanistan, subjected to torture and then transported to Guantánamo Bay. The Foreign Office denied it had any duty to press for the return of the two men, and a Foreign Office affidavit presented in court declared that 'a state making such a request may risk losing credibility with the state to whom it is made, such that it will not be taken seriously when it seeks to influence the behaviour of that state in relation to other matters of legitimate concern.' That statement was made in 2006 (consider how long we had, by then, been aware of US practices), and emphasised that 'the UK government attached considerable weight to public and private assurances from the US government that no torture is being practised at Guantánamo. The US is a close and trusted ally, with a strong tradition of upholding human rights.'

Britain did not want non-citizens back, even if the UK was the only safe place they could go: one of the men in question was a stateless Palestinian, the other an Iraqi national. There it would have ended but for an absurd error of judgment on the part of the intelligence services. Litigation for the two men, Bisher al-Rawi and Jamil el-Banna, was brought against the Foreign Office, the Home Office and the intelligence services; the first two responded in writing to deny the claim that they had demanded the arrest of the pair by the Americans. The intelligence services made no reply. 'Isn't that enough for your purpose?' one High Court judge asked lawyers representing the two men at an early hearing: 'Doesn't their failure to reply tell you all you need to know for your argument?'

The intelligence services then released telegrams they sent before the men's departure from the UK to Gambia, in the belief that the service would be exonerated since the telegrams did not carry the specific words 'please arrest'. Instead, the official messages stunningly demonstrated that the CIA had been tipped off by British intelligence that one of the men had been about to board a plane to Gambia carrying objects that could have been used as parts of an improvised explosive device (an entirely false assertion) and that they were involved in 'Islamic extremist' activity (also completely false). A later telegram, sent the following week when the men were on their way to Gambia, gave their date of travel and flight details, and was followed by a brief memorandum emphasising that neither would be given any UK consular assistance.

Refusing to the bitter end to acknowledge that wrong had been done, or that it would reverse its position in respect of non-nationals, the government nevertheless suddenly threw in the towel and requested the men's return, because it feared it would suffer a defeat in the House of Lords and have established against it a precedent it did not want for the future. And so it was that a handful of British residents came to be accepted for return. Had Mohamed been returned at that point to the UK on a flight from Guantánamo Bay together with the other British residents, and not had to fight for disclosure in the High Court to assist his defence before an ongoing military commission in Cuba, it would no doubt still remain the case that it would be his word against the British government's that he had ever been subjected to interrogative torture with the assistance of Britain in Morocco. After all, the Intelligence and Security Committee investigating that very issue behind closed doors in 2005, assisted by the intelligence services, had found no evidence at all to support the proposition.

The first to bring news from the dark side was Shafiq Rasul, who returned from Guantánamo in March 2004. Rasul relived his experience for an entire month in his lawyer's office, demonstrating to an illustrator with chains borrowed from a nearby market stall the forms of torture that he had endured in Afghanistan and then at Guantánamo Bay. By July 2004 he had produced a hundred-page illustrated account. Every aspect of his detention, every technique of torture used on him, is prohibited as a crime against humanity. Yet this, the first account made public from Guantánamo, would appear to have been entirely ignored by the Intelligence and Security Committee when in March 2005 it reported that it had reviewed two thousand interrogations in

Afghanistan, Guantánamo and Iraq by British intelligence agents who saw no evil, save for one who became aware that US interrogators were getting a detainee ready for interrogation by a process that appeared to involve 'hooding, deprivation of sleep' and making him stand in 'painful stress positions'. The committee stated that 'the treatment and holding conditions of these detainees by the relevant holding authorities are not within the remit of this committee', and pointed out that any individual complaints about treatment by MI5 or MI6 should be addressed to the Investigatory Powers Tribunal, a body created to sit entirely in secret. It is a curious detail that Rasul and his fellow British detainees reported that as they boarded the plane in Guantánamo to return to Britain, they were told by the Foreign Office representative accompanying them: 'Make sure you say that you were treated properly.'

Once we have arrived at a position where acquiescence in crimes against humanity by our government may well have occurred, the state can no longer demand that we acknowledge it as our protector and assert that in consequence the nation's security is at stake if secrets are revealed. This after all is the thesis on which the claim for secrecy is built. For years the government has sidestepped report after report on these issues by Amnesty International, Human Rights Watch, Justice, and Liberty, and has considered the interventions of those organisations as interventions of which it needs to take no note whatsoever. And for the past eight years the United Kingdom has shown a disturbing indifference to the criticism of international organisations. The European Committee for the Prevention of Torture conducted repeated checks on those interned indefinitely without trial between December 2001 and March 2005. Their observation that those being detained on secret evidence were being driven to madness was ignored; so too was the stinging critique of the European Commissioner for Human Rights. The government carried on with the detentions to the bitter end, months after the House of Lords had declared the legislation to be in violation of the fundamental provisions of the Human Rights Act. Similarly, the concerns the special rapporteur expressed in his report in 2009 appear to have remained unread. Is arrogance the reason that criticisms can never correctly apply to the UK? Are they only for others?

Although UN rapporteurs and UN committees carry (and should carry) authority and influence, without a mechanism for sanction they can be ignored. The European Court of Human Rights, however, commands a different position. The member states of the Council of Europe have a binding treaty commitment to the European Convention on Human Rights and to the court empowered to decide on state violations. In February 2009 the battleship 'UK Secret State' took a hit below the waterline when its system of secret courts considering secret evidence was held by the European Court to breach the rights of a number of applicants, in particular of access to information kept secret yet claimed to justify their detention on the basis of national security. This important decision is now beginning to play out in the myriad cases where it has been established that secret evidence has been used, many of which involve the sending of deportees to countries where they have been tortured in the past and will be tortured again. In 2008, the UN Human Rights Committee, reporting on the compliance of the UK with its human rights obligations, focused on what it saw, rightly, as our particular vice: secrecy. The Official Secrets Act, it stated, has 'been exercised to frustrate former employees of the Crown from bringing into the public domain issues of genuine public interest'. It recommended that state organisations should ensure that their 'powers to protect information genuinely related to matters of national security are narrowly utilised'. Similarly, the special rapporteur considered that the rule of law here is endangered by a power shift towards intelligence agencies that acts 'precisely to circumvent ... necessary safeguards in a democratic society, abusing thereby the usually legitimate secrecy of intelligence operations'.

Where we have got to is this: we have a state whose devices for maintaining secrecy are probably more deeply entrenched than in any other comparable democracy. We are condemned for what is already known internationally by the most authoritative of bodies about our activities in the past eight years, activities that are at the very least indicative of the most serious criminality, but to which we appear to be paying little or no heed. Our government's lawyers are fighting tooth and nail to preserve the secrets of the secret state, however disgraceful; to preserve them in large part because they would occasion disgust in the country at large, and not for the endlessly repeated formulaic claim that they will affect the safety of the realm or paralyse our legitimate democratic allies.

In fact, future attacks on our complacency now come potentially from all sides. In the US whistleblowers are a protected species; sooner or later a close relationship with a British friend will be revealed, perhaps even boasted about. The files covering the prosecutions of torturing interrogators in America are on the internet, officially released for all to see; the Senate Armed Services Committee 'shifted gear', and joined with the American

Civil Liberties Union to produce, with Obama's blessing, the last grisly details of what was already largely publicly known.

Gordon Brown was driven to announce that new standards would be set; but that was too little and it came too late. To protect ourselves for the future, we need to know what has occurred in the past. We cannot do it on trust. Investigations by the bodies empowered to act as our proxy have been triggered, if at all, by the accidental emergence of accounts from victims or their families, and will be allowed to tell us nothing. We need to know what the government and the intelligence services actually permit themselves and what they do not; it is said that MI6, if the orders are signed off by the foreign secretary of the day, can commit murder overseas. Is a foreign secretary's endorsement a defence in international law against a charge of participation in crimes against humanity? Clearly not: Nuremberg tells us as much. If the foreign secretary tells us that he has endorsed some form of participation in or encouragement of crimes against humanity committed by others, that cannot and does not keep him—or the prime minister—out of the dock in the international courts set up for that purpose. What is unsustainable is the belief that what we have been told is enough, and the willingness to accept that we are to be told nothing more.

May 2009

2

The Framing of al-Megrahi

It is, of course, now all about oil. Only a simpleton could believe that Abdelbaset Ali al-Megrahi, convicted of responsibility for the Lockerbie bombing, was not recently returned to his home in Libya because it suited Britain considerably to have him do so. The political furore has been very obviously contrived, since both the British and American governments know perfectly well the history of how and for what reasons he came to be prosecuted. More important, however, than the passing diplomatic storm is whether any aspect of the investigation that led to al-Megrahi's original conviction was also about oil, or dictated by other factors that should have no place in a prosecution process.

The devastation caused by the explosion of Pan Am Flight 103 over Lockerbie, at the cost of 270 lives, deserved an investigation of utter integrity. Article 2 of the European Convention on Human Rights demands no less. Where there has been a death any inquiry must not only be independent, but also effective and subject to public scrutiny, to provide the basis for an attribution of responsibility and to initiate criminal proceedings where appropriate. In its absence instead, a number of the bereaved Lockerbie families have of necessity themselves become investigators, asking probing questions for two decades without receiving answers. They have learned sufficient forensic science to make sense of what was being presented at al-Megrahi's trial and make up their own minds whether the prosecution of two Libyans at Camp Zeist near Utrecht was in fact a three-card trick put together for political ends.

Looking back, if the police investigation had been an entirely Scottish affair, with unrestricted access to all available information, without interference or manipulation from outside, perhaps the result could have been different. It is just possible, with a Scottish administration reeling from criticism heaped upon it both by England and the US for releasing the man convicted of the bombing, that a searching investigation conducted by a detached and truly independent enquirer, might restore to Scotland some integrity for the smallest force in the UK, the Dumfriesshire police, supported as it was by the selfless help and acute observations of the people of Lockerbie itself. Left to its own devices, it is arguable that Scotland might have achieved a very different target for suspicion and a very different conclusion. Instead, from the beginning, the investigation, and what were to become the most important aspects of the prosecution case against al-Megrahi, were hijacked by outsiders

Within hours of Pan Am 103's destruction, the countryside around Lockerbie was occupied: local people helping with the search under the supervision of Dumfries and Galloway police realised to their astonishment that the terrain was dotted with unidentified Americans not under the command of the local police.

Every criminal investigation in Britain has essential standards that must be met; if in any aspects of the investigation they are not, those should never in principle become the building blocks for a prosecution. There must be precise notes made of each physical exhibit found and by whom; its subsequent movements must be tracked; each time an exhibit is inspected, a record must be kept. The rationale is obvious: without a precise record, interference, contamination or simple mistake, could jeopardise the ability of a prosecutor to rely on evidence that is presented as tangible and therefore potentially more convincing. For that reason, a crime scene must be sealed off until searches are complete, by identifiable tape or by its notional equivalent.

Those engineering the destruction of a transatlantic airliner in mid-flight might have believed that it would be likely to happen over the sea. Instead, Pan Am 103 was destroyed over the Scottish town of Lockerbie and its fall-out was scattered over an area too vast to cordon off. The first and most desperate searches were for the passengers: could any have survived? Volunteers included a police surgeon from Yorkshire who had driven to the site as soon as he heard the news; together with the local police, he and others searched non-stop for twenty-four hours. They found bodies, none showing any sign of life; the doctor labelled each of the bodies he found, more than fifty of them, noting the place of discovery. Once it was clear there were no survivors, a search for evidence of the explosion's cause would begin.

Extraordinarily, however, unsupervised by the Dumfries and Galloway police, and without liaison with Lockerbie volunteers, scores of men, some wearing no insignia, some the insignia of the FBI and Pan Am (it was noted at the time that many of these men were clearly not Pan Am staff), invaded the area. Lockerbie residents searching for evidence under the supervision of their own police reported seeing unmarked helicopters hovering overhead, carrying men with rifles whose telescopic sights were pointing directly at them. And when, much later, items of baggage came to be married up with the passengers they had accompanied, there emerged disturbing signs of interference. The suitcase belonging to Major McKee (a CIA operative flying back to the US, reportedly to relay his concern that the couriering of drugs was being officially condoned as a way to entrap users and dealers in the US) was found to have had a hole cut in its side after the explosion, while the clothes in the suitcase were shown on subsequent analysis to bear no trace of explosives. A second suitcase, opened by a Scottish farmer, contained packets of white powder which a local police officer told him was undoubtedly heroin; no heroin was ever recorded as having been discovered. All but two of the labels that the volunteer police surgeon, Dr Fieldhouse, had attached to the bodies he discovered were removed and have never been found.

Although the crime was the most hideous Scotland had ever known, the integrity of the crime scene was violated. It was clear at the time that this was, in part, because outsiders were conducting a desperate search for wreckage that it was important for them to find and spirit away. As many police investigations over the years have demonstrated, such distracting irregularities can simply be red herrings, and these intrusions may have no bearing on the question of who blew up Pan Am 103. Was it individuals? Was it a country? And if so which one? From the very beginning, in fact, it seemed that the case could and would be easily solved. Considerable (and uncomplicated) evidence immediately to hand suggested who might be responsible; it was as if giant arrows were pointing towards the solution.

In the weeks before the bombing in December 1988 there had been a number of very specific warnings that a bomb would be placed on a Pan Am aircraft. Among them was a photograph of a bomb in a Toshiba cassette radio wired to a barometric timer switch; a number of such bombs had been found earlier that year in the possession of members of a small group with a history of successfully carrying out bombings, primarily of American targets. One group member, Marwan Khreesat, told police that five bombs had been made; at least one was missing at the time of the Lockerbie disaster and never recovered. The warnings were sufficiently exact that the staff of the American Embassy in Moscow, who usually travelled by Pan Am when they returned to the US for Christmas, used a different airline. Flora Swire, who was travelling to New York to spend Christmas with her boyfriend, found it surprisingly easy to buy a ticket.

The cassette bombs were built into electronic devices; one seized was built into a Toshiba cassette radio. When tested, each would run for something over thirty minutes from the time it was set. The utility of a barometric timer is that it cannot be activated until the plane is airborne; the bomb will not be triggered on the ground if the plane is delayed. Some seven or eight minutes would elapse as the plane gained height before the air pressure would drop sufficiently to activate a barometric timer set to go off thirty minutes later, i.e. thirty-seven or thirty-eight minutes after the flight took off. It was precisely thirty-eight minutes after Pan Am Flight 103 took off from Heathrow on 21 December 1988 that it exploded over Lockerbie; and when the remnants of the destroyed plane and its contents were put together piece by piece by the Dumfries and Galloway police, there was no question that the fragments discovered of a Toshiba cassette radio had housed the bomb.

Forensic scientists believed that the radio had been in a suitcase in which there were also clothes bearing a label that was traced to a shop in Malta. A search of the house of a man affiliated to the group that manufactured the Toshiba bombs produced clothes bought in Malta; it was established too that he had travelled to Malta before the bombing. And the owner of the Maltese shop from which the clothes were thought to have been purchased identified to his brother, without prompting, a newspaper photograph of the same man as someone closely resembling the person who had bought the clothes found in the suitcase loaded on to Pan Am 103 with the bomb inside.

With evidence of this kind, so unusually clear, why should there be any question of the safety of the conviction of al-Megrahi? Indignation emanating from the United States and from within the UK is surely justifiable?

But the man identified as having bought the clothes was not al-Megrahi, nor was he Libyan. The group making Toshiba radio cassette bombs had no connection at all with Libya. But neither the man nor the group was ever prosecuted for involvement in the Lockerbie bombing. The fact that the explosion took place exactly when one would have expected it to if a Toshiba cassette bomb had been used was ignored: the bomb had not, the prosecution contended at al-Megrahi's trial, been triggered by a barometric switch in this way. The Lockerbie device, it claimed, was different from the devices made by the group. The difference was that it was a Toshiba cassette radio with one speaker rather than two. From a logically compelling case that seemed to point clearly in one direction the prosecution switched tack, but not at the beginning: not, in fact, until two years after the bombing, when the politics of the Middle East shifted and new allies had to be found quickly if the flow of cheap oil were to continue.

It is not difficult to achieve a conviction of the innocent. Over many decades particular contributory factors have been repeatedly identified, and the majority of them are present, centre stage, in this case: achieving the co-operation of witnesses by means of a combination of inducements and fear of the alternative (the tried and tested method of obtaining evidence for the prosecution on which many US cases rely); the provision of factual certainty by scientists where there is no proper basis for it (a recurrent theme in UK as well as US convictions); reliance on 'identification' evidence which is no such thing. Add to that the political will to achieve a prosecution, and the conviction of the innocent was at the time of al-Megrahi's trial, and still is, easy. Fabrication demands outright dishonesty. However, it is not always necessary, or necessary in every aspect of an investigation: the momentum of suspicion, combined with a blinkered determination to focus on a particular thesis and ignore evidence pointing to the contrary, is a certain route to achieving the desired end. Al-Megrahi is reported as saying that he has evidence, which will be revealed on his death, that will prove his innocence. What can be looked at today fairly and squarely without the benefit of such a revelation, if it is to come, is already overwhelmingly sufficient to demonstrate that his was a very, very disturbing conviction in the first place. If there is to be an enquiry, the enquiry that is needed is one capable of establishing how it could ever have come about that an investigation that started with such clear and compelling evidence pointing in one direction came to be so distorted and manipulated to point eventually at Mr al-Megrahi and Libya.

Whether or not Libya was within the range of initial suspects, for the first two years there was no mention whatsoever of Libya.

The investigation originally proceeded on this footing, with clear evidence to hand of a motive (tit for tat retaliation); evidence of the existence of bombs intended to destroy airliners in mid-flight contained in the same brand of cassette radio discovered on the plane; and evidence implicating a Palestinian splinter group, the Popular Front for the Liberation of Palestine— General Command, which was prepared at the time to hire itself out to regimes that were known to be state sponsors of terrorism. Syria was one (somewhat earlier, Libya had been another), so too was Iran.

Behind every crime there is of course a motive. For the initial prime suspect, Iran, the motive was brutally clear. In July 1988 a US battleship, the *Vincennes*, shot down Iran Air Flight 655 in the Persian Gulf, with 290 passengers, many of them pilgrims en route to Mecca. There were no survivors. By chance a television crew was on the *Vincennes* when the attack took place and images of triumph at the carnage were immediately beamed around the world. When it became clear, as it did straightaway, that the attack was an appalling error, the US compounded its mistake: the president, Ronald Reagan, and the vice-president, George H. W. Bush, claimed self-defence and the ship's commander and crew were awarded high military honours, even though US commanders in adjacent battleships had already labelled the aggressive *Vincennes* 'Robo Cruiser', taking it upon themselves to piece together video footage of ships and interviews with crew members to demonstrate that George Bush's claim of self defence was a pack of lies.

Of course revenge was in the air. Two days after the downing of the Iranian airbus, Tehran Radio condemned the attack as an act of naked aggression and announced it would be avenged 'in blood-splattered skies'. At the same time, US Air Force Command issued a warning to its civilian contractors: 'We believe Iran will strike back in a tit for tat fashion—mass casualties.' Warnings became more specific: 'We believe Europe is the likely target for a retaliatory attack . . . due to the large concentration of Americans and the established terrorist infrastructures in place throughout Europe.' Within days, US intelligence was convinced that Iran meant business, and the CIA in due course acknowledged that it had intelligence that Ahmad Jibril, the leader of the PFLP-GC, had met government officials in Iran and offered his services.

Such a partnership would indeed have been ominous, since the activities of the PFLP-GC had since 1970 included planting bombs on planes—bombs built into transistor radios and detonated by a barometric pressure switch. It was in this context that the flood of warnings immediately preceding the disaster had obvious significance for the subsequent investigation. One of them read: 'team of Palestinians not associated with PLO intends to attack US targets in Europe. Time frame is present. Targets specified are Pan Am Airlines and US military bases.'

Five weeks before this warning, a PFLP-GC cell had been arrested in Germany. The PFLP-GC was precisely a 'team of Palestinians not associated with the PLO'. Jibril's right-hand man, Haffez Dalkamoni, was arrested in Frankfurt with a known bomb-maker, Marwen Khreesat, as they visited electrical shops in the city. In the boot of Dalkamoni's car was a Toshiba cassette recorder with Semtex moulded inside it, a simple time-delay switch and a barometric switch. Later US intelligence officials confirmed that members of the group had been monitoring Pan Am's facilities at Frankfurt airport. Dalkamoni admitted he had supervised Khreesat when he built bombs into a Toshiba radio cassette player, two radio tuners and a TV monitor. He said that a second Toshiba containing similar pressure switches had been built. Although Dalkamoni was prosecuted in Germany, in fact for an unrelated offence, Khreesat was inexplicably released; it only later became clear that he had been acting throughout as an undercover agent for Jordanian intelligence, an agency extraordinarily close to the CIA (which played a central role in its creation). On Dalkamoni's account, other bombs made by Khreesat were at large somewhere, including the one built into a second Toshiba player, which in turn Khreesat himself had confirmed.

On 9 November 1988 Interpol circulated warnings of evidence of unrecovered PFLP-GC bombs; the advice of the Germans was that as a priority airlines should be told. Heathrow Airport issued its own warning to security staff, stating that it was 'imperative that when screening or searching radios, radio cassette players and other electrical equipment, staff are to be extra vigilant'. Over the next three weeks the airport received more information, including photographs of the Toshiba bomb from the German authorities. (A document giving information and advice was drawn up by the UK's principal aviation security adviser on 19 December, but there were problems obtaining colour photographs and delays in the Christmas post and most airlines did not receive it until the new year, weeks after the disaster.)

In March 1989, less than three months after the downing of Flight 103, the then secretary of state for transport, Paul Channon, sat down to lunch with journalists. He talked, indiscreetly, of the brilliant detective work undertaken by the smallest police force in the country. Arrests, he told the journalists, were imminent. Although such conversations are customarily regarded as not for attribution, the temptation of a scoop led the next morning's newspapers to reveal that a cabinet minister had stated that those responsible for the Lockerbie bombing had been identified and would soon be arrested.

At precisely the same time, however, US President George Bush senior was reported by the *Washington Post* as having spoken to Margaret Thatcher about Lockerbie, advising her to keep Lockerbie 'low-key', to avoid prejudicing negotiations with Syrian and Iranian-backed groups holding Western hostages in Lebanon. There were no arrests; Channon left the cabinet; and the victim's families could by September 1989 observe the obvious: that political interest in the case and any desire to identify who was responsible for the disaster had disappeared. They demanded evidence that a proper inquiry was being conducted and in September 1989 Channon's successor, Cecil Parkinson, met the newly formed UK Families Flight 103. He, without any reservation, promised them a full judicial inquiry. Thatcher countermanded this promise, and he returned to the relatives with an admission of total failure. 'Low-key' meant no judicial inquiry, no prosecution, and instead a Fatal Accident Inquiry with no powers to subpoena which declined to investigate how the bomb got on the plane for fear of interfering with police inquiries.

As political players grow old, they reminisce and sometimes they forget what they are meant to have said or not said. Five years later Parkinson took part in a television programme about another horrific disaster, the sinking of the *Marchioness*, in which he confirmed that it was Thatcher who had blocked a judicial inquiry. He remembered discussing with the Lockerbie relatives whether, 'because the security services were involved', a High

Court judge could look into the security aspects and report privately to him: 'Because when you get into the Lockerbie business —how did we find out certain information, how did we know this, how did we know that?—you would have had to recall not only our own intelligence sources but information we were receiving from overseas. Therefore that had to be a closed area.' This then suggested the real block to a far-reaching inquiry: 'our own intelligence sources and others'.

Nevertheless, investigators had clearly remained confident that despite government diffidence a prosecution would soon be brought. Late 1989 produced once again the tantalising suggestion of an imminent arrest. The *Sunday Times* (known to enjoy detailed briefings from the police and security services) reported that the 'net was closing' on the Lockerbie suspects and stated categorically that the bombing had been carried out by the German PFLP-GC cell led by Dalkamoni under orders from Ahmad Jibril and with a bomb made by Khreesat. What was new was the suggestion that the bomb had first been put on a plane not in Frankfurt but in Malta. Clothes made in Malta, the report added, had been found in the suitcase in which police believed the bomb had been planted. A member of the Dalkamoni group, Abu Talb, who was then awaiting trial for separate offences in Sweden, had, it revealed, visited Malta. He was the man identified by the shop owner: the man who had clothes bought in Malta in his possession. The *Sunday Times* article went on to predict that Abu Talb would be extradited at any moment to stand trial for the bombing.

The suggestion that the bomb was placed on a plane from Malta was made in an attempt to marry up the finding of Maltese clothes with the already existing evidence of the German group.

As no passengers transferred from Air Malta to Pan Am 103A in Frankfurt, the feeder flight for Pan Am 103, then it would have had to be an unaccompanied bag from Malta that carried the bomb. Two documents were said to have been discovered: a list of the stages followed by Frankfurt airport's automated baggage system which related to Pan Am 103, and a handwritten work-sheet from one of the several stations from which baggage came into the system. As this was official information, it must have been given lock, stock and barrel by investigators to the journalist in question.

A fundamental objection to the last part of the new thesis was blindingly obvious: if the intended target was an American aircraft, why risk a premature explosion triggered by the barometric switch by putting the suitcase on an Air Malta flight? The scientific underpinning necessary to support a counter-proposition and the critical evidence necessary to provide a case against al-Megrahi was established during 1989 and 1990 and rested on two 'discoveries': a fragment of an entirely different type of timer in the remnant of a shirt collar and the matching of that fragment with the manufacturer's prototype. This timer, it was argued, could, once set, keep a barometric switch from detonating for days. It was in the development of this proposition that every safeguard fundamental to a criminal investigation came to be jettisoned.

That Iran and the PFLP-GC were responsible had, up to this point in time, fitted comfortably with UK and US foreign policy in the Middle East. Both countries had severed relations with Syria on the grounds of its persistent support for international terrorism; both had supported Iraq in the Iran/Iraq war, which ended in the summer of 1988. The obvious truth as it appeared at the time was that the Jibril group, sponsored on occasion by Syria, but in this instance by Iran, was a logical as well as politically acceptable fit.

Then, in August 1990, Saddam Hussein invaded Kuwait, thereby putting at risk almost 10 per cent of US oil supplies, and the stability of the Saudi and Gulf sheikhdoms on which the West depended to preserve the status quo in the Middle East. A sudden shift of alliances was essential: if Iraq were to be confronted, then Iran had to be treated differently and the Syrian regime needed to be brought on board. All else remained the same, but now Syria was an ally of the West and at the beginning of 1991 Syrians joined Western troops in the attack on Saddam Hussein's invading army.

By this time, Scotland had ceased to be the centre of gravity of the Lockerbie investigation. Now in charge was the CIA. Vincent Cannistraro, its chief of operations, had made his mark under Ronald Reagan with a clandestine programme to destabilise the Libyan regime. He boasted that he 'developed the policy towards Libya' which culminated in the bombing of Gaddafi's house in Tripoli in 1986 on the basis of intercept evidence later acknowledged to be false. Cannistraro shifted the investigation's approach. The suspect country was no longer Iran but Libya, and in November 1991, the UK and the US made a joint announcement that two Libyan Airlines officials, Abdelbaset Ali al-Megrahi and al-Amin Khalifa Fhimah, had planted the bomb in Malta on behalf of Libyan intelligence. Douglas Hurd, the foreign secretary, announced to the House of Commons that Libyans alone were suspected and that other countries were not implicated.

Years of protracted negotiations were to take place before agreement was reached that the Libyan government release the two men to stand trial in a 'neutral country'. It was not until May 2000 that the two Libyan Airlines officials who had run the airline's office in Malta finally went on trial—in a purpose-built court outside Utrecht created from a mothballed air-force base—under Scots law, albeit before three judges rather than a jury. What did Gaddafi expect when he agreed to the extradition of the two men? That they would in due course be exonerated because they were innocent but that he would meanwhile reap the diplomatic benefit by having delivered them? The idea of their individual responsibility was anyway bizarre. As agents of a state where not a mouse squeaks without the say-so of Gaddafi, al-Megrahi and Fhimah were either ordered to do what it was said they did, in which case dealing with Gaddafi as a statesman then and now has been beyond hypocrisy—or the thesis was wrong.

The key features needed to prosecute al-Megrahi successfully were the scientific identification of the circuit-board fragment, which would in turn establish its origin, and the identification of the purchaser of the clothes in Malta. The timers, the indictment stated, were made by a firm in Switzerland; their circuit board matched the fragment retrieved from Lockerbie, and they sold the timers exclusively to Libya. Everything, essentially, hinged on those links.

Who found the fragment? And who understood its relevance? Thomas Hayes of the Royal Armament Research and Development Establishment (RARDE) claimed the find (with his colleague Alan Feraday) and Thomas Thurman of the FBI claimed the analytical victory. All were swiftly hailed—or hailed themselves—as heroes. Thurman appeared on television on 15 November 1991, the day after indictments were issued against the two

Libyans, boasting that he had identified the piece of circuit board as part of a timing device that might have been sold to Libyan Airlines staff. 'I made the identification and I knew at that point what it meant. And because, if you will, I am an investigator as well as a forensic examiner, I knew where that would go. At that point we had no conclusive proof of the type of timing mechanism that was used in the bombing of 103. When that identification was made of the timer I knew that we had it.' This was the claim—the hard evidence—that linked Libyans to the crime. If the claim was false the bereaved Lockerbie families have been deceived for twenty years.

On 13 September 1995 the FBI's forensic department was the subject of a programme broadcast in the US by ABC. At its centre was a memorandum from the former head of explosive science at the FBI, Dr Frederic Whitehurst. It was a devastating indictment of a former colleague. The colleague was Thomas Thurman and the accusations related to his investigation of a terrorist attack in which a judge was killed by pipe bombs. Two years later, as a result of a review by the US inspector general, Michael Bromwich, into a large number of criminal investigations, Thomas Thurman was barred from FBI labs and from being called as an expert witness. Bromwich had discovered that he had no formal scientific qualifications and that, according to a former colleague, he had been 'circumventing procedures and protocols, testifying to areas of expertise that he had no qualifications in . . . therefore fabricating evidence'.

Thurman's contribution was the Libyan connection, and its plausibility relied on the accuracy of his statement that the fragment of circuit board proved that it would have been possible for the unaccompanied bag to fly from Malta without the otherwise inevitable mid-air explosion. And thus it was that a witness from Switzerland, Edwin Bollier, the manufacturer of the MEBO circuit board, was called on to provide evidence that such boards had been sold exclusively to Libya. Bollier was described by al-Megrahi's barrister in his closing speech as an 'illegitimate arms dealer with morals to match'. The evidence he was clearly intended to provide had begun to unravel even before the trial began. Sales elsewhere in the world were discovered, Thurman did not appear at the trial, and the judges commented that Bollier's evidence was 'inconsistent' and 'self-contradictory'. Other witnesses, they found, had 'openly lied to the court'. Despite all this al-Megrahi was convicted.

Bollier (whose evidence came to be obtained after weeks of FBI interviews) had been one of the most potentially dubious of many dubious witnesses for the prosecution. But Dr Köchler, the UN's observer throughout the trial, recorded that Bollier had been 'brusquely interrupted' by the presiding judge when he attempted to raise the issue of the possible manipulation of the timer fragments. Could the MEBO board, or a part of one, have been planted in such a way that it could be conveniently 'discovered'? After the trial, new evidence that would have been at the centre of al-Megrahi's now abandoned appeal made this suggestion more credible: a Swiss electronics engineer called Ulrich Lumpert, formerly employed by Bollier's firm, stated in an affidavit to Köchler that in 1989 he stole a 'non-operational' timing board from MEBO and handed it to 'a person officially investigating in the Lockerbie case'. Bollier himself told Köchler that he was offered $4 million if he would connect the timer to Libya.

There were throughout two aspects of the investigation over which the Scottish authorities exerted little authority: in the US, the activities of the CIA and in particular of Thomas Thurman and the forensic branch of the FBI; in England, the forensic investigations of RARDE, carried out by Hayes and Feraday. Without Hayes's findings, the Lockerbie prosecution would have been impossible. His evidence was that on 12 May 1989 he discovered and tweezed out from a remnant of cloth an electronic fragment, part of a circuit board. The remnant of cloth, part of a shirt collar, was then traced to a Maltese shop. A number of aspects of the original circuit board find were puzzling. The remnant was originally found in January 1989 by a DC Gilchrist and a DC McColm in the outer reaches of the area over which the bomb-blast debris was spread. It was labelled 'cloth (charred)' by the former, but then overwritten as 'debris' even though the fragment of circuit board had not yet been 'found' by Hayes. The fragment found by Hayes, and identified as a MEBO circuit board by Thurman, meant that the thesis of an Air Malta involvement could survive.

Even if one knew nothing of the devastating findings of the public inquiry in the early 1990s into the false science that convicted the Maguire Seven, or of the succession of thunderous judgments in the Court of Appeal in case after case in which RARDE scientists had provided the basis for wrongful convictions, Hayes's key evidence in this case on the key fragment should be viewed as disgraceful. There is a basic necessity for evidential preservation in any criminal case: every inspection must be logged, chronology recorded, detail noted. But at every point in relation to this vital fragment that information was either missing or had been altered, although Hayes had made conventional notes in respect of other exhibits he inspected in the Lockerbie investigation.

When he conducts his examinations, no forensic scientist knows whether or when there will be a prosecution that will depend on them. This makes it all the more important that his notes are exact. Hayes confirmed that it was his practice to draw pieces of circuit board where he found them—for instance in the vicinity of blast-damaged material—but he made no such drawings of this item, nor had he given it an exhibit reference number as he had done with every other exhibit being designated at the time, nor did he carry out a standard test for traces of explosive. Almost a month after his inspection of the timer fragment, Hayes was identifying and drawing exhibits which were given reference numbers smaller than the number of the vital exhibit. He recorded his finding on page 51 of his notes, but the pages originally numbered 51–55 had been renumbered 52–56 at some point. Hayes stated that he had 'no idea' when the change in pagination was carried out. The inference put to Hayes was that the original page 51 and the following pages had been renumbered, an original page removed and space made to insert what was now page 51 of his notes.

Curiously, a memorandum from Hayes's colleague Feraday to a detective inspector working on the case, written on 15 September 1989, referred to a fragment of green circuit board: 'Willy, enclosed are some Polaroid photographs of the green circuit board. Sorry about the quality, it is the best I can do in such a short time.' No one was able to explain why there should have been any shortage of time to make available in September 1989 photographs of an item that had been found on 12 May. Feraday's note continued: 'I feel that this fragment could be potentially most important so any light your lads or lasses can shed upon the problem of identifying it will be most welcome.' Again no one was able to explain what light the lads and lasses could shed on something it was most curious they had not seen before now, given that Hayes had recovered it in May. Clearly it could not have been seen by the police before the cloth was passed to Hayes at RARDE and the fragment extracted by him. If the exhibit had been properly photographed, as was normal practice, then Feraday would not have needed to rely on Polaroids of dubious quality. The issue of his notes' pagination was described by Hayes as 'an unfathomable mystery'. In view of the importance of exhibit PT/35(b), how could the court have been satisfied by this evidence? The new evidence of the former MEBO employee who stole a circuit board would of course have been ripe for analysis by the Court of Appeal, which has now been discharged from considering new evidence in al-Megrahi's lately abandoned appeal.

A secondary important proposition for the Crown to consider was that the suitcase was on the second layer of a luggage container on the aircraft—which meant that it must have come from Frankfurt. Examining the largest surviving fragment of the outside case of the Toshiba device on 25 January 1989, Hayes had considered its state consistent with its having been at the base of the container. This would have contradicted the Crown's position that the device was in a suitcase that had arrived last, as unaccompanied baggage from Malta via Frankfurt, and so was nearer the top. By the time he gave evidence at the trial, Hayes had revised his assessment of its position.

(Since the trial, evidence new to the defence but known from the start to the police has surfaced of a break-in at Heathrow in the hours before the disaster. The Fatal Accident Inquiry, without this knowledge, had made a finding in 1991 that Pan Am

103 was 'under constant guard at Heathrow'. Iran Air's hangar at Heathrow was next to Pan Am's.)

How have we heard of Hayes before, or Feraday? Among the many wrongful convictions in the 1970s for which RARDE scientists were responsible, Hayes played his part in the most notorious of all, endorsing the finding of an explosive trace that was never there, and speculating that a piece of chalk mentioned to the police by Vincent Maguire, aged sixteen, and a candle by Patrick Maguire, aged thirteen, 'fitted the description better' of a stick of gelignite wrapped in white paper. Both were convicted and imprisoned on this evidence, together with their parents and their uncle Giuseppe Conlon, who was to die in prison. All were later found to be innocent.

Although Feraday was often addressed, uncorrected, as 'Dr' or 'Professor' when he gave evidence, he had no relevant academic qualifications, only a higher national certificate in physics and electronics some thirty years old. Dr Michael Scott, whose evidence has been preferred in appeals to that of Feraday, commented that 'the British government employed hundreds of people who were extraordinarily well qualified in the areas of radio communication and electronics. Alan Feraday is not qualified yet they use him. I have to ask the question why.' Feraday, like his US counterpart Thurman, no longer appears as an expert witness, but he had already provided the key evidence in a roll-call of convictions of the innocent. A note of a pre-trial conference with counsel prosecuting Danny McNamee (who was wrongly convicted of involvement in a bombing in Hyde Park) provides a typical instance: 'F [Feraday] prepared to say it [a circuit board] purely for bombing purposes, no innocent purpose.' The implication here was that anyone who had involvement with this circuit board would have knowingly been involved in bomb construction. That, in common with many other assertions made by Feraday, was entirely false, but it resulted in McNamee's imprisonment for eleven years.

To discover that al-Megrahi's conviction was in large part based on the evidence of scientists whose value as professional witnesses had been permanently and publicly demolished ten years before his trial is astounding. The discovery nearly two decades ago of a large number of wrongful convictions enabled by scientific evidence rightly led to demands that the community of forensic scientists change its ways. Similarly, a series of catastrophic misidentifications required the introduction of sound new practices for evidence based on that most fragile of human attributes, visual memory. Witnesses must not be prompted; a witness's memory, as far as possible, must be as safely protected from contamination as a crime scene. The first description is vital. If a witness makes a positive identification of one individual, no subsequent identification of a second is permissible. Equivocation and uncertainty are not enough. Even if the science that convicted al-Megrahi had not offended against every minimum standard, then the second pillar of the prosecution case, his identification by Tony Gauci, the Maltese shopkeeper, would remain spectacular in its noncompliance with any safeguard. His descriptions of the man who bought clothes included these observations: '6'0'' ' (al-Megrahi was 5'8''), 'fifty years old' (he was thirty-seven), and 'hefty'; he 'had been to the shop before and after', 'had been there only once'; he 'saw him in a bar months later'; he would 'sign statement even though I don't speak English'; al-Megrahi 'was similar but not identical', 'perhaps like him but not fully like him', and, fatally for any identification of al-Megrahi in the first place, that he was 'like the man in the *Sunday Times*' (in other words, like Abu Talb, whose picture Gauci had initially identified). But Gauci's evidence was needed and, reports suggest, handsomely rewarded. He is reported as now living in Australia, supported by millions of US dollars.

That a court of three experienced judges convicted on such evidence and that an appeal court upheld the conviction is profoundly shocking. Köchler, the UN observer, reported finding the guilty verdict 'incomprehensible' in view of the court's admission that Gauci's identification was 'not absolute'. We had come to believe that such an outcome, resting on invalid identification, was no longer possible. 'The guilty verdict', Köchler wrote, was 'arbitrary, even irrational' with an 'air of international power politics' present 'in the whole verdict', which was 'based on a series of highly problematic inferences'. He remarked on the withholding of 'substantial information' ('more or less openly exercised influence on the part of actors outside the judicial framework') and on the very visible interference with the work of the Scottish prosecutors by US lawyers present in the well of the court. But most seriously, he set out his 'suspicion that political considerations may have been overriding a strictly judicial evaluation of the case'. All of this harks back to the bad old days when a blind eye was turned to the way convictions were obtained and to the mantra, often repeated, that there was no such thing as a political prosecution.

Al-Megrahi's trial constituted a unique legal construct, engineered to achieve a political rapprochement, but its content was so manipulated that in reality there was only ever an illusion of a trial. Dr Köchler recorded at its conclusion that it was 'not fair' and that it was not 'conducted in an objective manner', so that there were 'many more questions and doubts at the end than the beginning'. Since then, these doubts have not disappeared: on the contrary, the questions are graver, the doubts have grown and so has the strength of the evidence on which they are based. Köchler's observations continue to have compelling relevance. He found the respect of the court, the defence lawyers included, for the 'shrouds of secrecy' and 'national security considerations' to be 'totally incomprehensible to any rational observer'. 'Proper judicial procedure,' he continued, 'is simply impossible if political interests and intelligence services—from whichever side— succeed in interfering in the actual conduct of a court.'

The term miscarriage of justice carries with it the inference of accident, but also of death. There is a pressing need to investigate in detail how it has come about that there has been a form of death in this case—the death of justice—and who should be found responsible.

September 2009

3

Was It Like This for the Irish?

As commentators and participants write their own histories of thirty years of conflict in Northern Ireland, they sometimes, with hindsight, provide a description which could be read as a coherent, albeit stumbling progression towards an inevitable and just conclusion. The raw anger, pain and despair that was the reality of those years becomes muted.

Muslims, the new suspect community in this country, ask if their experience today can be compared with that of the Irish in the last third of the twentieth century. Muslim prisoners in Belmarsh, Long Lartin and beyond, and others equally confined in many different ways with their families beyond prison cells, have already noted the similarities of that conflict and of its injustices and search for some hope of a similar progression.

But it is dangerously misleading when we look to the recent past for lessons for the present to acknowledge the many terrible wrongs in Northern Ireland's recent history and yet to assert that it was the conflict in Northern Ireland that produced them. It was instead injustice itself, again and again, that created and fuelled the conflict. To map its thirty-year trajectory is to discover that before Bloody Sunday, when British soldiers shot and killed thirteen unarmed Catholic demonstrators who were marching

to demand not in fact a united Ireland but equal rights in employ-
ment, education and housing (as well as an end to internment),
the IRA was a diminished organisation, unable to recruit. After
Bloody Sunday, overnight volunteers from every part of Ireland
and every background came forward. Throughout the years of
bloody armed conflict, every lawless action on the part of the
British state provoked a similar reaction: internment, 'shoot to
kill', the use of torture (hooding, extreme stress positions, mock
executions), brutally obtained false confessions and fabricated
evidence. All of this was registered at the time by the community
most affected, while the British public, in whose name these
actions were taken, remained ignorant: that the state was seen to
be combating terrorism sufficed.

Central to the anger and despair that fuelled the conflict was
the realisation that the British courts would offer neither protection
nor justice. The Widgery Report into Bloody Sunday, carried
out by the lord chief justice, absolved the British army and
backed its false account of thirteen murders, ensuring that for
thirty years Irish nationalists would see the legal system as
entirely aligned against them. The Saville Inquiry, a decade-long
re-doing of Widgery's fatal contribution, will never be a substi-
tute for what should have existed: an appreciation of the danger
that injustice, small or large, can create combined with the understanding that this danger is nowhere more acute than when the
courts cannot or will not provide a remedy.

This should be always in our minds as we analyse the experiences of our new suspect community. Just as Irish men and
women, wherever they lived, knew and registered every detail of
each injustice as if it had been done to them, long before British
men and women were even aware that entire Irish families had

been wrongly imprisoned in their country for decades, so Muslim men and women here and across the world are registering the ill-treatment of their community here, and recognising, too, the analogies with the experiences of the Irish.

As good a place as any to begin is 19 December 2001. On this date a dozen men, all foreign nationals, were interned in this country. Recognising the connotations of the word 'internment', discredited and abandoned in Northern Ireland, the government insisted this was not equivalent to arbitrary detention without trial, a practice forbidden by the European Convention on Human Rights except in extreme emergencies, because each man was free to leave. The premise on which he was detained was that the United Kingdom could not in fact send him back to the one place he could go, his country of origin, since it was accepted that he would be without question a target for torture, if he was not killed on arrival.

December 2001 did not in fact mark the beginning of Britain's official interest in men described as 'Islamists', since some from Egypt, Jordan, Tunisia, Libya and Algeria, all here as refugees, had long been the subject of complaints to the UK by the regimes they had fled. Immediately after 9/11, however, Tony Blair professed an unashamed desire to stand 'shoulder to shoulder' with President Bush.

It would have been difficult to match Bush's executive onslaught on constitutional rights in the US, by means of the Patriot Act; the designation of 'enemy combatants' and their detention by presidential order; the abolition of habeas corpus; the subjection of detainees to torture in Afghanistan and Guantánamo or their unofficial outsourcing via rendition flights to countries specialising in even more grotesque interrogative practices, many of them those same regimes which had long pressured the UK to take action against their own dissidents. Claiming that a parallel emergency faced Britain, Blair bulldozed through Parliament a new brand of internment: indefinite detention without trial for a dozen foreign nationals. The 'evidence' was to be heard in secret with the detainee's lawyer not permitted to see the evidence against him and an auxiliary lawyer appointed by the attorney general who, having seen it, was not allowed to see the detainee. The most useful device of the executive is its ability to claim that secrecy is necessary for national security. Each of the dozen men snatched from his home on 17 December 2001, and delivered to HMP Belmarsh, expressed astonishment: first at finding himself the object of the much trumpeted incoming legislation and, second, at discovering who also had been detained. Each asked why, if he was suspected of activity linked to terrorism, he had never been questioned by police or the Security Services before it was decided that he was a 'risk to national security'. The sole activity which some speculated might be the reason for their detention was their attempt to support Chechens when in 1999 their country was the subject of a second brutal invasion by Russia. But thousands of others had acted similarly, and such support was not unlawful.

Each man was told that, for a reason that could not be disclosed, he was in some unspecified way thought to be linked to unspecified persons or organisations, in turn linked to al-Qaeda, which was then depicted by now discredited 'al-Qaeda experts' as taking the form of the hierarchical pyramid of conventional Western structures. At the base of the pyramid were those who had been interned, almost all of whom said that they had never heard of al-Qaeda before 11 September 2001. This initial experience carried echoes of other wrongful detentions, little different from the clumsy evidence of the West Midlands police who coerced an innocent Irishman, John Walker, into confessing that he was an IRA 'brigadier', ignorant of the fact that such a title existed only in the British army. This confession was nevertheless swallowed whole. Walker, one of the Birmingham Six (detained only because they were Irish and Catholic), spent sixteen years in jail before the assertions of their prosecutors were finally discredited.

There should have been no need for the Muslim community to anticipate years of anguish before an inquiry told society what their community already knew, since just before Christmas 2005, three and a half years after internment had been rushed through Parliament, the House of Lords gave its judgment on that legislation in what should have stood as the most important legacy of British law in recent history. The law lords swept aside what had been argued by the attorney general to constitute a just system necessary to uphold national security. Focusing on the government's disproportionate response to a claimed emergency, and its indefinite detention only of foreign nationals, the language of the law lords was heroic in its strength and there was on its delivery a recognition that the ruling's importance went far beyond the twelve detainees, eight of whom had now been driven into mental illness, four of those into florid psychosis, and had been transferred by the home secretary from Belmarsh to Broadmoor. (The very name of the prison in which the detainees were held had by then become a shorthand for injustice.)

After the judgment, however, signalling as it did that the government had impermissibly crossed the legal barriers guaranteed by domestic and international treaties, it became clear that the government intended to ignore the spirit if not the letter of the decision. It had also become clear that the government had, and continues to have, a wider strategy of which internment legislation was only one part. Little by little, ripples of information found their way to the surface, sometimes confirmed by the government, sometimes denied. While the world knows and can assess for itself what chains of reaction were created by the wars in Iraq and Afghanistan and by the enormity of injustice suffered by the Palestinians, the cumulative effect of many other policies deserves analysis and concern.

It emerged for instance that in late 2001 the UK had begun to tip off other governments, for the ultimate benefit of the US, about the whereabouts of British nationals and British residents around the world. Moazzem Begg, living with his wife and children in Pakistan, was seized by unknown kidnappers in January 2002; within hours he was in the hands of Americans but with a British intelligence agent to hand, and transported without any semblance of legality to Bagram, a former US airbase in Afghanistan, now adapted to be an interrogation camp perpetrating torture. After a year during which he witnessed the murders of two fellow detainees, he was moved to isolation and brutality in Guantánamo Bay. Until he finally returned to this country in 2005, nothing was known of the presence, soon after his lawless abduction, of a British agent. Instead, for the whole of that year in Bagram, the Foreign and Commonwealth Office looked his father in the eye and said that they had no information whatsoever about his son and that the Americans would tell them nothing.

Seemingly unrelated areas of injustice, we learn, have all along been connected. Two British residents, acknowledged to have been seized in 2002 in the Gambia and subjected to rendition by the US as a direct result of information provided by British intelligence, were for the next five years subjected to interrogation (including torture) very specifically to obtain information about one of the men interned in Britain. Meanwhile another of those interned in December 2001, a Palestinian, trying to guess the reason for his detention, told his lawyers that he had raised money for many years to build wells and schools and to provide food for widows and orphans in Afghanistan. One of those wells, he said, bore the name of the son of its donor, Moazzem Begg. The Palestinian's lawyers, knowing by now that Begg was in Guantánamo, started for the first time to think the unthinkable. In the court for internees, the Special Immigration Appeals Commission, there is a brief opportunity for the detainee's lawyer to question an anonymous Security Service witness concealed behind a curtain, before the lawyer is asked to leave the court so it can continue its consideration of secret evidence. The witness was asked: 'Would you use evidence that was obtained by torture?' Unhesitatingly the answer was that it would be used. The only issue that might arise, the agent added, would be the weight such evidence should be given. Three years after this, in December 2005, the House of Lords affirmed the principle that no English court can ever admit evidence derived from torture, no matter how strong the claimed justification or emergency. The message for the government was again unequivocal: the principles of legal obligation must be adhered to in all circumstances.

The closing of the sorry chapter of internment takes us, sadly, back to its beginning. On the surface at the time, one saw only the strength and intended permanence of the rulings of the House of

Lords. Underneath, however, and unseen, was the fiercest of undertows dragging in reverse. Today for the Muslim community, any protection that may come from the courts is viewed in the context of what has occurred since 2005, as constituting only the most temporary of impediments before the government implements new methods of avoidance, and where it views its legal obligations as irritating interferences with an overarching quest for claimed national security.

After three months of prevarication, the internees were released on bail under stringent conditions, whilst the Home Office was simultaneously pushing a second tranche of emergency legislation through Parliament, this time to introduce control orders which demanded of the now released detainees a substantial number of obligations, any breach of which would constitute a criminal offence carrying a penalty of up to five years' imprisonment. Three of the detainees, including the Palestinian, were pitch-forked out of Broadmoor during the night and driven by police to empty flats. One of them, a man without arms, was left alone and terrified, unable to leave the flat or to contact anyone without committing a criminal offence, subject to a curfew and allowed no visitors unless approved in advance by the Home Office. Two of these three detainees were immediately readmitted to psychiatric hospitals; neither of them had been hospitalised before being interned. One wonders how psychiatrists could effectively treat refugees, victims in their home countries of unspeakable torture, who had been detained for three and a half years under legislation declared, finally, unlawful. A number of psychiatrists seeing individual men whose faith forbids suicide and from cultures where acknowledgement of mental illness is uncomfortable found patterns of psychological damage explicable only as a result of their indefinite detention without trial. Could those men now, out of prison but under the restrictions of control orders, ever achieve a semblance of normality?

After five months of compliance with control order obligations a number of men, albeit out of prison, were observing the most disturbing of effects, in particular if the released detainee was married and with children.

The electronic tag the men were obliged to wear, which registered every entry and exit from the house, was only one element of a family's altered existence. A voice recognition system, used to confirm the detainee's presence at home during curfew, was activated by machines, of US manufacture, which often failed to recognise the accents of Arabic speakers, with the result that uniformed police officers would enter the house in significant numbers at all times of the day and night. No visitor would come near their homes because to enter required first to be vetted by the Home Office. Children whose coursework at school involved the internet could not meet the school's requirements. The use of the internet was forbidden. Families had endlessly to involve lawyers in the most trivial matters: to obtain permission to go into the garden; to attend a parent-teacher meeting; to arrange for a plumber to enter the house.

What has become of these men? Are they still, years later, trying to live normal lives despite the restrictions? The answer was to come quickly, only five months after their release. On 7 July 2005 bombs exploded in the London underground. Within days it was known that the bombings had been carried out by young British men born and bred in Yorkshire. However, on 5 August Blair announced that 'the rules of the game have changed' and that diplomatic agreements were being achieved to

deport the same small group of detainees to their countries of
origin, although the government knew that the use of torture was
still routine in these countries. An assurance, it was said, would
now be obtained that the men themselves would not be tortured
after they were returned, and an independent monitoring organisation in each country would guarantee that the assurance was
being adhered to. Nevertheless, these deportations flew in the
face of two important legal commitments to which this country is
obliged to adhere: one, to send no person to a country where
there is a risk to him of torture, the central premise of the Refugee
Convention; and, two, to achieve the eradication of torture (and
not by negotiating a single exception, while offering no protest to
a regime's continuing use of torture on others).

On 11 August the Algerian and Jordanian former internees
were again arrested. There were soon more arrests, this time of
two Algerians who had been acquitted unanimously in a trial at
the Old Bailey in April 2005 of involvement in a conspiracy to use
ricin, an allegation that had been seized upon at the time of their
original arrest by Colin Powell in his attempt to justify the invasion of Iraq to the UN. (One juror described how for him a
moment of truth came early in the trial, when a witness from
Porton Down nervously drank three containers of water while in
the witness box seeking to explain why an early lab report said to
have been conveyed to the police and confirming that there was no
trace of ricin, had, curiously, never reached the cabinet office.)

Those detainees who remain in the United Kingdom are still in
prison or under extreme bail restrictions. One has been returned
twice to Broadmoor from prison before being bailed to a psychiatric hospital. There are now two more Jordanian detainees and
several Algerians, while Libya rapidly became the third state to

promise safe re-entry to its dissident citizens. As for the promised monitoring organisations, one was purpose-built in Jordan in 2005, a husband and wife team bankrolled by the UK, which by the summer of 2007 (when two thousand inmates in one Jordanian prison were beaten the day after the first ever visit of an NGO, Human Rights Watch, to whose representatives they had complained of torture), had still never visited a prison. In Libya, the independent monitor agreed to by Britain was the Ghadafi Foundation, headed by Colonel Ghadafi's son.

Algeria never did fulfil Blair's pledge of a comprehensive memorandum of understanding with Britain, nor did it appoint an independent monitor, although both safeguards were said by him to be non-negotiable precursors to any deportation. Constant prevarication was ascribed initially to the Algerian president's ill-health, and then to meetings being postponed, until finally the detainees' appeals against deportation could be delayed no longer. SIAC, hearing evidence in large part in secret, found that Algeria's 'body politic' appeared to have moved to 'a state of lesser danger' for perceived dissidents, that a limited amnesty was on offer, so that the refugees would not be put on trial, and thus that it was safe to deport them. Several Algerians in prison here or under severe restrictions decided to return. As they said in a letter to a British newspaper: 'We are choosing the alternative of a quick death in Algeria to a slow death here.'

In making this decision, two of the Algerians, Benaissa Taleb and Rida Dendani, dramatically miscalculated. Astonishingly, SIAC allows secret evidence to be given even on the issue of an individual's future safety. Had the men properly understood the reality (or more important the fragility) of diplomatic arrangements, perhaps neither would have made his fateful decision to return. Each was told that an amnesty applied in Algeria which he should sign even though he had committed no offence; indeed special arrangements were made by the Home Office for each man to have bail to attend the Algerian Embassy in London for this purpose. Each believed that he would not be detained more than a few hours on arrival and that, as the British diplomat organising these deportations had promised SIAC, there was no risk that he would be held by the infamous DRS secret police. In fact both were interrogated by the DRS for twelve days, during which time they were threatened and subjected to serious physical ill-treatment. They were then charged, tried and some months later convicted, on the basis of the 'confessions' forced from them during this time. Dendani was sentenced to eight years' imprisonment, Taleb to three.

At the heart of Britain's reassurances as to their safety had been its repeated confidence that the Algerian state would place too high a value on its relationship with Britain to risk its disapproval. No British official has ever attempted to visit either man in prison, despite reports that both continue to be held in conditions that violate every international norm. No official attended their trials, and the fact that visa applications by the men's UK lawyers have been ignored by the Algerian authorities, despite repeated requests for help from the British government, has been commented on with amusement during proceedings before SIAC as evidence of Algeria's independent spirit. A desperate letter describing how he had been tortured was sent by one of the men from prison in Algeria to the president of SIAC. It brought no response. Despite all this, it is still maintained that it is safe to deport people to Algeria. An application on behalf of appellants for a secret hearing at which information given to lawyers by those afraid of providing it in the open could be properly and safely examined was rejected, not because SIAC considered the proposal without merit, but because the court's rules, it appears, do not allow for such a procedure.

Is the treatment of these two men simply a blip in an otherwise safe and lawful process? Is it reasonable for the wider Muslim community to see significance beyond those two individual experiences whose fate has gradually been pieced together so that it has now become clear that Britain has secretly been willing to disregard the most basic principles of refugee protection. First, we learned that Taleb's interrogation by the DRS was indisputably based on information received by the Algerians from the UK. Not only did Algeria possess the 2003 findings against him by SIAC (under the internment legislation that the House of Lords subsequently held to be unlawful), but it now has been discovered that the asylum claims of possibly all of this small group of detainees have been passed to the regimes from which they had fled. Asylum rests on the central premise of confidentiality, and a clear promise to that effect is given by the Home Office to all those who claim asylum in Britain. After all, the contents of the application, or the very fact of its having been made, might create danger for the applicant if he returned to his country of origin. In the case of one man whose appeal against the Home Office's request to deport him has not yet been considered by SIAC, it has been discovered (and admitted by the government) that a specially commissioned medical report describing his vulnerable condition was prepared here by Belmarsh Prison and sent to Jordan.

Taleb, known throughout his internment only by a letter of the alphabet so that his family in Algeria would not be at risk, arrived there to find that all the information about him based on secret evidence under now abandoned legislation was held by the Algerians, un-anonymised. As Taleb had decided to return to Algeria in the hope he would be safe, no court in Britain had considered his deportation case, yet the Algerians possessed all the British government's 'evidence' about him. His subsequent trial confirmed his worst fears. His Algerian lawyers argued, and he gave evidence of this himself, that he had signed an unread 'confession' after spending twelve days in DRS custody and after having been beaten by his interrogators. The presiding judge countered by referring to the 'West' and its 'illusory democracy': 'Weren't you imprisoned, confined to your home for several years without trial, without charge and without respect for any procedure of either inquiry or investigation in a democratic country par excellence, Great Britain? No one in this court can teach us a lesson or put to us the least complaint on this matter, since in this country no person has been subject to such treatment.' The judge saw Taleb's claim for asylum in the UK as amounting to a 'betrayal' of his country of origin. Asylum was accorded 'only to those who hated their own country', and the judge commented at length on Algerians who had gone abroad and painted a black picture of the country's human rights situation 'to the benefit of NGOs whose time was spent vitiating the truth about Algeria'.

Taleb's eventual conviction in Algeria was, curiously, for going to Afghanistan in 1991 to fight the Russians. He had, in fact, travelled to Pakistan in 1991 as an idealistic eighteen-year-old, where he taught refugees from Afghanistan; the Russians had left two years earlier. As for the amnesty he had signed at the Algerian Embassy in London before he voluntarily left Britain not only its relevance but its existence was now denied. The

United Kingdom displayed no interest in any of this. The reality is that British Petroleum has sunk £6 billion into obtaining oil from Algerian southern Sahara; the US and the EU are scrambling with the UK for a slice of Libya's economic potential; and Jordan, one fifth of whose annual national income is provided by the US, is content to act as its most reliable provider of safe destinations for rendition and torture.

A recent judgment published by the European Court of Human Rights (in the case of a Tunisian whom Italy sought to deport, although Tunisia continues to practise torture) revealed that the UK had tried to intervene in the case in the hope of undoing one of the European Court's most important decisions, *Chahal v. UK*. In that case, the court insisted that the claim of a risk to national security could never trump a European country's international obligation not to return a refugee who might be tortured. The European Court rejected the UK's attempt at intervention in uncompromising terms.

Yet through a myriad other routes Britain has continued to attempt to evade internationally recognised legal restraints. When several years ago Tony Blair attempted to deport an Egyptian human rights lawyer who had been the victim of truly terrible torture in his own country, he argued that an assurance from Egypt of the man's safety would suffice. Unusually, during a court challenge to the legality of his detention, private memoranda between Blair and the Home Office were made public. Across a note from the Home Office expressing concern that even hard assurances given by Egypt were unlikely to provide real protection against torture and execution, Blair had scribbled: 'Get them back.' Beside the passage about the assurances he wrote: 'This is a bit much. Why do we need all these things?' The man succeeded in his court challenge, but later, on the basis of secret information provided by Egypt, he was made the subject of a UN Assets Freezing Order managed by the Treasury. He has no assets, no income and no work, and can be given neither money nor 'benefit' without a licence. 'Benefit' includes eating the meals his wife cooks. She has required a licence to cook them, and is obliged to account for every penny spent by the household. She speaks little English and is disabled, so has been compelled to pass the obligation onto their children, who submit monthly accounts to the Treasury of every apple bought from the market, every bus fare to school. Failure to do so constitutes a criminal and imprisonable offence. In the House of Lords, Lord Hoffman expressed horror at 'the meanness and squalor' of a regime 'that monitored who had what for breakfast'. But the number of such cases now multiplies daily. They have nothing at all to do with national security. They only succeed, as they are intended to, in sapping morale, and they have everything to do with reinforcing the growing belief of the suspect community that it is expected to eradicate its opinions, its identity and many of the core precepts of its religion.

In December 2001 it was a small group of foreign nationals who paid the price for Blair's wish to show solidarity with the US, and their predicament has never been widely known or understood beyond the Muslim community. But joining them in prison today are more and more young British men, and occasionally women. Many have little or no idea why they are there, although, even more disturbingly, the majority have been tried by the courts in conventional trials before conventional juries. Why is it, therefore, that the accused do not seem to comprehend why they are there when the prosecution has in any trial to serve all of its evidence in the form of statements, in order to inform the defendant of the case against him? The answer is that the vice underlying the internment/deportation cases is now being perpetrated in conventional trials. The accusations are similarly inchoate: defendants are said to be 'linked to terrorism' or 'linked to extremism and/or radical ideology'. In these cases, the evidence before the court has time and again been found after a search on a defendant's computer or in a notebook; the defendant is charged with possession of a certain item or this item is held to demonstrate the defendant's desire to incite, encourage or glorify terrorism.

The right to a fair trial is in many ways difficult to articulate. If a defendant believes his or her prosecution is unjust, does he or she have any concepts to hang onto that are not entirely nebulous, unless they can prove, as those wrongly convicted in Birmingham or Guildford did, that their confessions had been brutally coerced? Or in the case of Judith Ward, when it was proved that the prosecution had withheld for eighteen years evidence that disproved her claimed fantasies; or that of Danny McNamee, in which the information that circuit boards identical to those he was held to have used were in the possession of an actual bombmaker was kept from his defence and a fingerprint was claimed to be his when it was not. In each of these cases, bad, misleading and on occasion false 'expert' evidence also played its part. Less well-known guarantees of a fair trial do, however, exist, just as clear protections for refugees exist, which were equally intended to hold good for all time and in the face of all emergencies. The relevant provisos, which underpin the right to a fair trial, are that the law should be clear and certain so that individuals can be confident that their behaviour does not transgress the limits society has set; that the application of the law should never be retrospective;

and that there are protections intended to preserve freedom of speech, religion, thought and privacy. Young Muslims search the internet in their tens of thousands, as do non-Muslims. Any internet search, however, leaves an ineradicable trace which can and does provide material that puts its searcher at risk of prosecution for possession of information that might be 'of use to terrorists'. They even risk arrest for writing anything that could be said to 'incite' or 'encourage' 'terrorism'.

This is the context of many current prosecutions. The fruits of a police search are uncovered, prosecutions mounted for the 'possession' of literature, films and pamphlets bought or viewed on websites, even if that viewing was swift and the item discarded or even deleted. The defendants are stigmatised as potential terrorists and their cases considered by juries more often than not without even one Muslim among their ranks to provide what the concept of twelve jurors randomly selected is intended to contribute to the trial process—a reflection of the collective good sense of the community.

In 2007 two young Muslim women were separately tried at the Old Bailey for having written works deemed by the prosecution to serve a terrorist objective. One was the 'Lyrical Terrorist', whose appeal against conviction was eventually upheld in June 2008. The other, Bouchra el-Hor, was acquitted by her jury; she had the good fortune to have as a defence witness Carmen Callil, who witheringly described the letter that el-Hor had written as a classic example of the way devout women, whether Catholic or Quaker, Puritan or Muslim, experiment with creative writing as a means of expression while living isolated existences. The jury laughed at Callil's savage critique, but one could see recognition and understanding follow.

This is very dangerous territory, however, where a lucky accident of interpretation is critical to a jury's understanding of a case and where police and prosecutors, neither of them armed with any understanding of Islam, press on with prosecutions although the court struggles properly to understand what is at issue. Where the human story is straightforward, the task is far easier, but even so, now that secret accusations and secret courts have intruded into the sacrosanct forum of an open jury trial in which secrecy is not allowed, what is a jury to make of an allegation that a defendant has breached a control order imposed on the basis of secret evidence which holds that he is a risk to national security? On trial just before Christmas in 2007 was a young Essex Muslim, Ceri Bullivant, who had been placed under a control order and then charged with a criminal offence when he absconded, unable to cope with the restrictions of that order. In his case the jury magnificently acquitted him on the basis that he had a reasonable excuse to breach his order. It was only later, however, in the High Court, that what lay behind the secrecy became suddenly clearer. Mr Justice Collins quashed the order itself; before he did so, an intelligence agent giving evidence from behind a screen admitted that the tip-off which had led to the decision that Bullivant was a risk to national security and 'associated with links to terrorists' had come from a friend of Ceri's mother who, after drinking heavily, had phoned Scotland Yard, which failed ever to contact the caller to ask for further explanation. Equally disturbingly, a childhood friend of Bullivant's told the court that he had been approached by MI5 officers and asked to spy on local Muslim youths. When he pointed out this was unlikely to be productive since he was not himself a Muslim, he was encouraged to become one and told that 'converts are given a special welcome.'

From a distance such blundering negligence might seem merely laughable, but those affected by it feel resentment, anger and despair. Why should young people as much a part of Britain as any other citizen require what are in effect interpreters to establish their innocence? The more religiously based the evidence, the greater the opportunity for obstinate incomprehension. Conspicuous by its absence in case after case is any evidence, expert or otherwise, proffered by the prosecution that attempts to explain the most basic concepts of Islam to a non-Muslim jury. Take the instance of a saying of the Prophet Muhammad familiar to all Muslims: 'Fight the unbelievers with your wealth, yourselves and your tongues.' Should a man who made a supplication in those terms in Regent's Park Mosque on the holiest night of Ramadan, in support of the citizens of Fallujah who were that night defending their city in the face of the announced eradication by US troops of all who remained there, have anticipated that he might be breaking the law, or that he could be charged and prosecuted in 2008 after a friend's home video of his prayer was found by police in a raid? He had, after all, repeated those same challenging words many times over the years, and explained again and again to the public, to the police and politicians, one of the most fundamental concepts of Islam, the Ummah, which makes every Muslim anywhere in the world the brother of every other Muslim, so that if one is attacked others are obliged to help. Should he be surprised to be prosecuted for having reiterated these same words of support in a mosque? The answer lies in Blair's warning: 'The rules of the game have changed.' Previously accepted boundaries of freedom of expression and thought have been redefined and are now being prosecuted in effect retrospectively, with the result that our criminal justice system is becoming further distorted as many truly innocent defendants plead guilty, against their lawyers' advice, terrified by the prospect, as they see it, of inevitable conviction and ever lengthening prison sentences. Thousands of others, all of whom have searched the internet, watch with horror the process of criminalisation and punishment.

In this country we did not grow up with a written constitution, and human rights legislation entered our law only recently. In times of tension we struggle to find answers to basic questions. Are there rules and can they be changed? Are there legal concepts that protect a community under blanket suspicion, or should that community's adverse reaction to suspicion be seen as oversensitivity in the face of perceived political necessity? Should we accept the concept of the greatest good for the greatest number? The answer is again the same: we are bound by international treaty and, belatedly, by domestic human rights legislation, to hold that there are inalienable rights that attach to the individual rather than society. Article 8 of the European Convention protects not only respect for family and private life, but also the individual against humiliating treatment; Article 10 protects freedom of expression; Article 9 freedom of thought, conscience and religion; and Article 14 guarantees that in the enjoyment of these rights any discrimination is itself prohibited. Occasionally, fierce campaigning successfully sounds an alarm: the proposed extension from twenty-eight to forty-two days of the time allowed for questioning those suspected of involvement in terrorism was energetically and publicly fought. But there are less obvious erosions of parallel rights.

If this is indeed how it was for the Irish, we should urgently try to understand how significant change came about for them. Much current reminiscence ignores vital factors, such as the inescapable responsibility of the Irish Republic and, above all, the political weight of the Irish diaspora and the far-sightedness of those who began and maintained contact, long before Blair was elected and claimed the ultimate prize. Throughout the thirty years of conflict, forty million Americans of Irish descent formed an electoral statistic that no US administration could afford to ignore. It is said that on the night before he decided to grant a visa to Gerry Adams, Bill Clinton watched a film about the catastrophic injustice inflicted on one Irish family by the British state. Here, Lord Scarman and Lord Devlin, retired law lords, joined Cardinal Hume, the head of the Catholic Church in England, in educating themselves in the finest detail of three sets of wrongful convictions involving fourteen defendants. At one critical moment Cardinal Hume confronted the home secretary, Douglas Hurd, challenging the adequacy of his briefing.

No similar allies for the Muslim community are evident today, capable of pushing and pulling the British government publicly or privately into seeing sense. Spiritually, the Muslim Ummah is seen as being infinite, but the powerful regimes of the Muslim world almost without exception not only themselves perpetrate oppression, but choose to work hand-in-hand with the US and the UK in their 'war on terror'. It is for us, as a nation, to take stock of ourselves. We are very far along a destructive path, and if our government continues on that path, we will ultimately have destroyed much of the moral and legal fabric of the society that we claim to be protecting. The choice and the responsibility are entirely ours.

April 2008

4

Are We Our Brothers' Keepers?

During the first months of this year, the embers of a long-burning legal controversy reignited in the United States, fuelled now uncontrollably by politics. 'Of all the issues,' Rahm Emanuel was warned by Republican Senator for South Carolina Lindsey Graham, 'this is the one that could bring the presidency down.'

The 'issue' concerns whether and where to try several dozen Guantánamo prisoners, in particular Khalid Sheikh Mohammed, described as the principal architect of 9/11, and four of his alleged co-conspirators. Bolted onto the primary debate as to whether they should be tried in a military commission or in a federal court are two further propositions, the first described by Bush administration lawyers as 'the obvious solution, don't bother trying them at all', and the second, that there should be no funding for the civilian criminal trials of persons suspected of involvement in terrorism.

In January 2010, the Obama administration decided that five Guantánamo prisoners, including Khalid Sheikh Mohammed, would be tried in the New York Federal District Court in Manhattan, that six would face military commissions in a place yet to be decided, and that at least forty-eight others (the number is undoubtedly higher) should be held indefinitely without charge. Obama had asked US Attorney General Eric Holder to take the decision, 'in an effort to maintain an independent Justice Department', but is now reported to be involved himself, recognising that his administration had miscalculated the political fallout. Graham's objective? To reach a deal with the White House over the attorney general's head; trading Republican support for the closing of Guantánamo in exchange for a military trial for Khalid Sheikh Mohammed.

At stake is not just whether Khalid Sheikh Mohammed and his co-conspirators receive a civilian court trial but the legal fate of all terrorism suspects, the future of the Guantánamo Bay detention facility and the credibility of the US Attorney General Eric Holder. This is dangerous terrain, for politicians as well as for lawyers.

Portrayed as a battle between US constitutionalists who argue for jury trials and hardliners who want no such thing for men accused of terrorism, this debate exposes serious fault lines in the protections constitutionalists contend would be in place if 'civilian justice' rather than that of the military were achieved for those suspects. For a start, so determined a political involvement in ongoing court proceedings must erode any claim to a clear separation between the judicial and executive branches of state in the US.

This battle comes on the eve of decisions in the European Court of Human Rights in Strasbourg on the extradition of a number of men whose cases led a court in London six years ago to state that no suspect should ever be extradited to the US if there were any risk that he might face trials of the sort now being argued for there. But by a curious roll of legal dice, not just the issue of military commissions, but of many of America's basic criminal justice practices, how and where it tries the accused, how it obtains evidence, how it prosecutes and how it treats its prisoners, have all since 2004 been exposed to investigation first by courts in London and then in Strasbourg. This scrutiny has been made necessary because the US wants to try a number of men, many of them British, but whose extraditions from the UK have been frozen while the courts determine whether there is a serious risk that sending them to the US would be to deliver them up to flagrantly unfair trials, severe and prohibited ill-treatment, or the death penalty.

In the white heat of 9/11, Cheney, Rumsfeld and Bush were able to conduct a blitzkrieg on the concept of due process as they ransacked the world in search of suspects. In justification of their actions, they conjured up new legal definitions. An 'enemy combatant' was any individual judged to be actively aligning himself against America; and 'military commissions' in turn were constructed to deal with combatants thus defined. In parallel, America's appetite to extend its conventional jurisdictional reach grew.

A number of individuals arrested in the UK were astonished to learn that activities they had undertaken years before could have offended against US law. Two of those individuals, Babar Ahmad and Syed Talha Ahsan, had before 9/11 contributed in the UK to a website which several years later came to be construed by US prosecutors as having supported the Taliban at a time when it was the de facto government of Afghanistan. The accused men's misfortune was that the service provider for the website was located in Connecticut and thereby subject to US jurisdiction. A third suspect, Haroon Aswat, had in 1999 spent two weeks on a farm in Oregon, a location, it was suggested, that was a military training camp for Muslims (it was no such thing) where Muslims were reputedly headed to receive military training (they never did). Two more, Adel Abdul Bary and Khalid al-Fawwaz, one of whom had received, in 1998, faxes in an Islamic information office in London reporting that two US Embassies in East Africa had been bombed that day, were charged with conspiring to cause those explosions. All these individuals discovered with equal astonishment that the basic propositions put forward by the US prosecutor in their cases had a further unexpected and dire consequence; they fell into a category created by President Bush to deal with the 'worst of the worst'.

In each case, the extradition court at London's Bow Street swiftly found that the extraditee, by virtue of the breadth of the US definition, 'would meet the criteria which would permit the president of the United States to make an order designating the defendant as an enemy combatant', and thereby liable to be tried by a military commission. A military court, even if its proceedings were identical to those in a civilian trial, cannot meet the mandatory European Convention requirement of judicial independence. Its judges are military employees within a hierarchical structure headed by their commander-in-chief, the president; there is therefore no separation of powers between the executive and the judiciary.

As a result, the extradition judge at Bow Street court went on to decide that if any individual who risked designation as an enemy combatant were to be extradited to the United States, he would lose his due process rights to a fair and public trial before an independent tribunal; if, the judge concluded, a man could be detained 'subject to Military Order No. 1', probably in Guantánamo Bay, where he could be held indefinitely, he would be 'deprived of his European Convention rights and extradition would be barred'.

At this point the extradition requests would have been refused but for a flurry of diplomatic exchanges, in which the US Embassy in London assured the UK government that the defendants would not be prosecuted before a military commission, nor treated as enemy combatants: they would instead be tried before a federal court 'in accordance with the full panoply of rights and protections that would otherwise be provided to a defendant facing similar charges'.

It has been in large part on the vexed question of the value of diplomatic assurances and their limitations that each of these extradition cases has been considered first by the extradition court at Bow Street, then on appeal to the High Court in London. Ultimately, the UK's decisions fall to be externally judged decisively, in Strasbourg, by the sometimes exacting standards of the European Convention on Human Rights, where these extradition cases have now been stalled for nearly three years. Could an unenforceable diplomatic promise hold good, in law or in practice, after the men had been extradited? And what action, if the men were tried before a jury and acquitted, might the US then take if it nonetheless believed the defendants constituted a threat?

The concept that its own conformity with international legal principles should be exposed to any outside judgment is entirely alien to America. When, for instance, Jordan refused to endorse exemption for Americans from trial in the International Criminal Court for crimes against humanity, the US threatened immediately to withdraw its contribution of one-fifth of Jordan's annual budget. The Jordanian parliament promptly revoked its decision.

More than half a century after the nation-states of the world committed themselves to a significant chain of treaty obligations intended to permit external scrutiny of their internal compliance with those treaties, America continues to maintain a remarkable isolationism. It opts out, not of the treaties themselves, but of the provisions that permit inspection and sanction—the teeth of enforcement. While it is a party to the UN Convention Against Torture, it has never ratified the treaty's optional protocol, nor does it accept the right of individual petition to the Committee for the Prevention of Torture. In those countries which have signed up, successive UN special rapporteurs on torture carry out unannounced inspections intended to penetrate the facade of impressive constitutions on whose face no violation of the rights of any individual could occur. They dig out grim truths and their reports are often biting and always public. Nor does America accept the application of its own regional American Convention on Human Rights, which it signed but never ratified. Thus no individual in the US can have recourse to the Convention's enforcement body, the Inter-American Court on Human Rights. While petitions can be sent to the Inter-American Commission on Human Rights, the reports of the Commission are not binding and its findings are consistently ignored.

Although some US commentators give Obama credit for attempting to demonstrate that the executive branch can wage war while also respecting the limits imposed on presidential power by the rule of law, that is not how it appears to the outside eye. When in February 2009 a federal judge overseeing the cases of Guantánamo detainees asked whether the new administration wanted to modify the Bush position that the president could imprison people indefinitely without trial, Obama's Justice

Department maintained that it could if those persons were part of al-Qaeda or its affiliates or their substantial supporters. This was precisely what the extraditees and their lawyers had argued would be the case, first before the UK courts and then in Strasbourg; strong jurisprudential doubt emanated from US lawyers as to whether any diplomatic note could bind the hand of any future US commander-in-chief if national security were perceived to be at stake in years to come.

In an interview with the *Washington Post*, the US attorney general acknowledged the possibility that trials may be switched to military commissions, and attempted to rationalise the position: 'At the end of the day, wherever this case is tried, in whatever forum, what we have to do is ensure that it is done as transparently as possible and with adherence to all the rules. If we do that, I'm not sure the location or even the forum is as important as what the world sees as proceeding.' In fact 'what the world sees' is generally of little consequence. The US is accustomed to filtering out external opinion; it will judge for itself whether or not it has 'adhered to all the rules' since it exempts itself from sanction when the politically driven choices it makes fail to comply with international minimum standards.

External observers, including the men arrested on warrants for extradition to the US (as well as defence lawyers within the US and no doubt many prosecutors too), watched with alarm in the years after 9/11 as Jose Padilla, a US citizen, and Ali Saleh al-Marri, a Qatari student in the US, were moved back and forth between conventional criminal trials before juries and military detention. (In a naval brig in Charleston the detainees found themselves subjected to the same ill-treatment as others in secret sites around the world.) Although at least one senior State

Department lawyer, Harold Koh, maintains that the new administration's changes mean that the United States can now claim its national security policies are fully compliant with domestic and international law under 'common and universal standards, not double standards', the administration, unnerved by the political backlash, returns to the uncertainties of the days of Padilla and al-Marri, and beats a hasty retreat from its insistence on civilian trials, and is considering indefinite detention without trial. Perhaps most disturbingly of all, it seems not to appreciate that in the US almost every basic safeguard necessary to achieve a conventional fair trial for the accused has in practice been long ago abandoned or destroyed.

Neither nation-states nor their courts are accustomed to stand in each other's way when a request for extradition is made concerning a person described, however inappropriately, as a 'fugitive'. Extradition arrangements originated in the ancient world as a practical way of demonstrating courtesy and goodwill between sovereigns, the first known instance between a pharaoh of Egypt and the king of the Hittites. The language of our government and our courts is equally deferential today, emphasising the necessity of 'effective relations between sovereign states' as well as bland assertions such as 'It goes without saying that [the United States] will be true to its constitution'. But the assurances given by the US since September 2001 should have been greeted with considerably more scepticism. Twice the British foreign secretary has had to come before Parliament to apologise, explaining that US assurances to the UK concerning rendition had been false; and in 2008 the Select Committee on Foreign Affairs recommended that US assurances should no longer be accepted, given the country's continuing denials that its interrogative practices met the universal definition of torture.

No assurances at all, fragile or otherwise, are on offer to protect against the spectre that extraditees, even if acquitted, might be subjected to rendition or indefinite detention, or the grim reality of solitary confinement in a small sealed cell in a US prison before and after trial, or against sentences that could amount to a hundred years or the prisoner's natural life. Nor are assurances offered that such treatment, or the threat of it, will not be used to force guilty pleas from the innocent as well as a promise to 'co-operate' in providing evidence with which to prosecute others. While still in the UK, more than one extraditee has been visited by a US prosecutor armed with a copy of the *Federal Sentencing Guidelines*; 'These', it is explained (sentences of more than any man's natural life expectancy), 'are the facts of life.' The lawyers of one young man, Gary MacKinnon (alleged to have hacked into Pentagon computers), offered the opportunity of a guilty plea, were told that should he refuse, once in America he would 'fry'.

Guilty pleas resolve 97 per cent of US trials, an extraordinary statistic inevitably achieved by the defendants' apprehension of what lies ahead—not just for the 'worst of the worst'—and a desire to avoid, at any cost, the US law's most extreme application.

Each extraditee can picture himself, once in the US, in the position of those witnesses for the prosecution he now sees ranged against him. It is loudly denied that improper pressure is exerted to secure the co-operation of witnesses to make the prosecution's case, but why then does the plea agreement for the main (and only) cooperating witness against one extraditee, Haroon Aswat, contain the provision that were he to cease cooperating 'the

United States would be free to exercise all rights it may have to detain the defendant as an enemy combatant' and to return him to total isolation under SAMs, the much feared Special Administrative Measures? And why did the cooperating witness's attorney, in communications with other lawyers which form part of the extradition court's record, write (before his client had agreed to give evidence against others), 'As it turns out, one of the key witnesses against my client is a British citizen who's being held at Guantánamo Bay as an enemy combatant.' Thus the dominoes fall one by one. Later, flippantly, after the London court's decision in 2005 the same attorney wrote again:

> It's pretty apparent the good guys were winning until the diplomatic note showed up. What a pity. I did find ... aspects of the ruling especially entertaining ... that the Magistrate somehow thinks a diplomatic note stating that the US won't try this guy in military court will bind the president. Since when has our president—the greatest international scoffflaw of our time—ever felt bound by any diplomatic accord?

For two of those awaiting extradition, Adel Abdul Bary and Khalid al-Fawwaz, there is an additional irony. The US charges them with involvement in the East Africa bombings, and they have had an acceptance in a London court by a lawyer on behalf of the US that a military commission does not provide a fair trial, and an assurance that they will not be subjected to one. They have watched with astonishment what has happened nevertheless to their co-accused, Ahmad Ghailani, who, it is now proposed, will be tried with them in Manhattan and whose pending trial will, the authorities claim, have 'a two-pronged effect; justice will be done and the credibility of the courts will be re-established'.

In the summer of 1998 Ghailani was indicted for involvement in the East Africa bombings, and the New York Federal District Court issued a warrant for his arrest. In January 2005 his captors in Pakistan reported that he had been handed over to the United States 'several months ago'. He was being held as a ghost prisoner in a secret CIA-run prison. Reported by Human Rights Watch to be one of the significant 'disappeared', he finally emerged in 2006, but not in the Manhattan court. Instead, on precisely the same factual allegations contained in the indictment issued by the New York Court in 1998, he was placed on trial before a military commission in Guantánamo Bay, where charges were filed by military prosecutors for the bombing of the US Embassy in Tanzania. 'Officials were aware of the 1998 civilian indictment,' their spokesman, General Hartmann, explained, 'but were proceeding with a military case at Guantánamo. That is the avenue the president, the Congress and the Department of Defence established' he said 'to deal with alleged war crimes in connection with the global war on terror'. Each development in Ghailani's case served to reinforce the parallel ongoing contention of his co-accused in the UK as to the fragility of US assurances in their case, and to confirm their worst fears. Their co-defendant had been ordered to be tried within a system specifically constructed to remove from him that 'full panoply of rights' assured to them as well as to prevent access to him. The United States and its president (not a divisible entity for the purpose of the United Kingdom's responsibilities towards extradition) had chosen to split the trial, half of which—Ghailani's half—was to be conducted in Guantánamo in secret session and outside the conventional rule of law in the US.

Ghailani's position was, however, to change yet again. In the spring of 2009 he was moved from Guantánamo into the civilian court system and transferred to New York to stand trial before the Federal District Court in Manhattan. Meanwhile, deep into its consideration of the extradition cases in Strasbourg, the European Court asked the UK government: 'If extradited, approximately how long would the Applicants spend in pre-trial detention?' A simple response was given: the US constitution guarantees the right to a speedy trial. But what of Ghailani, who had disappeared into a secret prison in 2004, and did not surface for trial until five years later and only then after the abandonment of plans to try him before serving soldiers at Guantánamo Bay? His lawyers in New York assert that instead, in those years, he has been submitted more than a hundred times to techniques 'amounting to torture' and that 'he appears to be so damaged' by his treatment that his ability to assist his lawyers in preparing his defence has been harmed.

From the perspective of the European Convention, the future of the extraditees begins to appear as not just political but legal pandemonium too. The guarantee that each will enjoy a fair trial, dependent as that concept is on a number of separate fundamental principles, is already in grave doubt. There is, significantly, no reticence in America in commenting upon an arrest, a trial, or the evidence that the prosecution claims loudly, from the outset, to possess. In the UK the inhibiting and perhaps strangulating Contempt of Court Act demands that any reporting that might influence a jury be prohibited; the flurry occasioned by arrest and charge, even in the most dramatically newsworthy cases, is silenced until the trial begins. In the US the reverse is the case; the concept of freedom of speech permits free-ranging commentary and unlimited coverage. The decision to move Ghailani to the

Manhattan court drew sharp attacks and acted as the precursor of the current political storm. On 10 February 2010 the *New York Times* reported Ghailani's prosecutors stating without inhibition that the delays in bringing Ghailani into the criminal justice system were justified on national security grounds and 'did not violate his speedy trial rights'. The prosecutor added further that Mr Ghailani was a long-standing al-Qaeda terrorist 'who was initially treated as an intelligence asset after his capture'. 'The United States was, and still is, at war with al-Qaeda,' the prosecutor said. Where in all of this sorry history is the presumption of innocence, guaranteed by the UN Declaration of Human Rights? Where is there any regard for the US constitutional right to a fair and speedy trial? Where is there respect for the concept of trial by a jury free from prior knowledge or opinion?

Each nation creates its own system of justice. For the European Court of Human Rights, required to address cases from forty member states, each with a different system (some are inquisitorial, with an investigative *juge d'instruction*, others adversarial; some have lay juries, others professional judges) achieving a case law of precedent and setting minimum standards through its jurisprudence for Article 6 of the Convention (the right to a fair trial) is more problematic than meeting other minimum norms. Nevertheless, even in a system in which a professional judge makes the ultimate determination, there are taboos concerning public commentary. When in one case a French government minister and the prosecutor publicly asserted the guilt of a defendant, Patrick Allenet de Ribemont, France was held by Strasbourg to have breached his right to a fair trial. How then to achieve a fair trial in the US where it is open season for commentary on every accused, and where the very fact of entitlement to a trial at all in these cases is the most bitterly fought of ongoing political battles just as much for members of any potential jury pool as for politicians?

European courts have often had to consider cases just as challenging as those that it is currently argued merit no due process in the US. Abdullah Ocalan, the Kurdish leader of the PKK, kidnapped in Kenya by Turkish intelligence agents, was as prized a 'high value detainee' by Turkey as is Khalid Sheikh Mohammed by the US. Once captured, Ocalan was held in complete isolation, and his first hearing was held before a panel of three judges, one of them a Turkish military officer. At the trial that followed he was convicted and sentenced to death. The presence of the military officer (although jettisoned before Ocalan's full trial) and the isolation to which he was subjected before he stood trial caused the Strasbourg Court to find against Turkey; his right to a fair trial guaranteed by Article 6 of the European Convention had been irretrievably violated by pre-trial isolation and by the military presence, and that in turn vitiated all claims to legitimacy the sentence of death could thereafter have. His conviction could not stand.

Forced to investigate conditions in the US, and to enlist the help of hard-pressed defence lawyers there in establishing otherwise unreported data, extraditees have come to understand that practice after practice is accepted as standard in America that, in Europe, could risk the prohibition of a trial, or if the trial took place, subsequently cause its nullification. So too could European minimum standards bring to an end widely used US conditions of imprisonment. Within a system of criminal justice that for all of us, from a lifetime of watching procedural dramas, seems more familiar than our own, there are profoundly disturbing features which do not accord with the assumptions we continue to maintain, despite the actions of the previous administration, about the strength and permanence of the constitution of the United States.

Not every shortcoming, we discover, can be explained as a product of the Bush/Cheney assault on due process rights or a reflection of their enthusiastic embrace of coercive ill-treatment as an investigative tool—issues that US lawyers, civilian and military, have in the last decade combined in force to protest alongside campaigners. Rather, many ugly practices have been long embedded in the US criminal justice system and their opponents have largely lacked the strength or resources to mount a collective and sustained resistance, or to achieve the endorsement of US court rulings national or international, in their favour.

American lawyers advise us, with weary resignation, that principles we believed prevailed there as here do not have any sound footing in US case law. Evidence obtained from a prosecution witness by coercion, for instance, cannot be excluded before a jury hears it. A senior counsel representing the United States in the High Court in London explained that US law permits the otherwise unlawful kidnapping of suspects elsewhere in the world, in order to bring them 'to justice' in the US. And every defence lawyer who has provided witness evidence for the benefit of the Strasbourg Court regarding clients held in isolation pending trial in the US speaks of the bleak hopelessness of the defendant, the deterioration of his mental state and of the impotence of lawyers over many years in achieving redress. Those who represent Muslim defendants convicted of involvement in terrorist activity predict with certainty that none will ever escape from the most extreme forms of isolation that American prisons can impose.

We read, year after year, obscene details of American executions in the US: descriptions of frustrated attempts, hour after hour, to find the vein of a prisoner sufficient to take a lethal injection. For a long time, the UK had no cause for complacency; it abolished capital punishment in 1965, but nevertheless continued to extradite to countries that retained the death penalty, and would have carried on so doing had not the European Court determined in 1989 in the case of *Soering v UK* that the 'death row' phenomenon, in which a person might spend years awaiting execution in the US while the legal process was exhausted, constituted inhuman and degrading treatment according to Article 3 of the Convention. Since then no European state has been permitted to extradite in the absence of an assurance that conviction would not invite the death penalty.

But what of extradition to a future of total isolation? Can we comfortably, and within the law, contemplate sending people to that fate instead? Some of those men who currently await extradition are imprisoned in a small unit, where they are at least in the company of other human beings; they can talk, argue, study, cook, write, paint, or exercise outdoors in whatever sunlight imprisonment in Worcestershire may afford them. This is not luxury. It is, of course, deprivation, of family life in its entirety, of freedom and of hope. But once on American soil each man has been told by US prosecutors to expect to face total isolation—under Special Administrative Measures until trial and then, upon his anticipated conviction, solitary confinement in a Supermax prison, ADX Florence in Colorado, potentially for life and without any prospect of parole. He will be confined in a cell seven feet by twelve feet, with a moulded concrete bunk; his food will be delivered through a slot in the door; external communication, even with a doctor, will come via a closed circuit television in his cell. For one hour in each twenty-four, he can visit a small adjacent dark pit where he can exercise alone. He will be imprisoned (although he will not see them) among 'the most severely psychotic people' that the most experienced analyst of the effects of Supermax confinement, Professor Terry Kupers, has seen in twenty-five years of psychiatric practice, and will thus be likely, since the primary cause is isolation, to become one such himself. His solitary confinement can, and perhaps will, continue for life.

After his tour of the US in 1842 Charles Dickens wrote of the use of isolation in the American prisons he had seen, stating, 'I hold this slow and daily tampering with the mysteries of the brain to be immeasurably worse than any torture of the body.' He wrote:

> I am persuaded that those who devised the system of prison discipline and those benevolent gentlemen who carry out its execution do not know what it is they are doing. I believe that very few men are capable of estimating the immense amount of torture and agony which this dreadful punishment, prolonged for years, inflicts upon the sufferers; and in guessing at it myself, and in reasoning from what I have seen written upon their faces, I am only more convinced that there is a depth of terrible endurance which none but the sufferers themselves can fathom and which no man has the right to inflict upon his fellow creatures.

By the late nineteenth century, evidence of the devastating effects of solitary confinement on prisoners' health had surfaced, and in 1890, the US Supreme Court, considering the case of a death row prisoner, echoed the language of today's doctors: 'A considerable number of the prisoners fell, even after a short confinement, into a semi-fatuous condition, from which it was next to impossible to arouse them and others became violently insane; others, still, committed suicide.' But whilst in the nineteenth century, isolation was intended to provide an opportunity for the redemption of the prisoner's Christian soul, Supermax prisons have now re-emerged in the US from a different perspective and no longer that of the well-intentioned 'benevolent gentlemen' of Dickens's encounters. Penologists argue that in the late twentieth century many politicians and members of the public began to indulge a powerful 'rage to punish'. Craig Hainey, one of those penologists, describes a punishment wave having swept over the US with such force that it ripped citizens, politicians and courts from the ethical moorings that had once served to restrain the severity of criminal sanctions. Hainey believes that, as a nation, the US now celebrates and often demands—rather than lamenting or merely tolerating—official cruelty and the infliction of pain in its criminal justice system. What once passed for 'penal philosophy' now amounts to little more than devising 'creative strategies' to make prisoners suffer. Supermax confinement, built on the twin pillars of prolonged solitary confinement and extreme severity of conditions, is one of those strategies. Very distant from Dickens's forgiving criticisms that those who devised the system of solitary confinement did not know what they were doing, every detail of today's cells is carefully designed by architects to limit access to natural light, to eliminate stimulation or distraction, and to reflect a total disregard for the principle that all prisoners are members of the human community. Although in 1995 one US District Court judge, in the case of *Madrid v. Gomez*, described conditions in a Supermax unit as pushing at 'the outer bounds of what most humans can psychologically tolerate and in the case of mentally ill prisoners, does mean the equivalent of placing an asthmatic in a place with little air to breathe', no constitutional bar to their continuing use has been imposed by any court.

It is undoubtedly on the issue of solitary confinement, before and after trial, more than any other, that American prisoners pay the price for their country's determined isolationism. Even Denmark, a country considered by the UN special rapporteur on torture to be entirely compliant with its every other human rights obligation, was warned following an in-country inspection that to detain a suspect in solitary confinement, if it were done in the expectation that it might induce an admission of guilt, could constitute torture contrary to Article 3 of the European Convention. The same special rapporteurs have expressed their particular concern about conditions in detention in US maximum security prisons which equally violate internationally protected rights, but they can do no more than register concern from the outside since they have no right to conduct internal inspections. Despite a stream of authoritative critiques and recommendations by the UN Human Rights Committee that the US government should scrutinise conditions in Supermax prisons and implement minimum UN standards, there have been no changes, there has been no scrutiny, and the federal government is building ever more of the same facilities. Human Rights Watch informed the world as long ago as 2000 that in the US there were nearly 20,000 prisoners in complete isolation, nearly 2 per cent of the prison population who 'typically spend their waking and sleeping hours locked in small sometimes windowless cells sealed with solid steel doors. A few times a week they're let out for solitary exercise in a small enclosed space with almost no access to any source of mental stimulation and assignment to such prisons is usually for an indefinite period.' Today, official estimates suggest a total twice that of a decade ago.

To date, the few judicial honours that can be awarded for facing up to the issue of confinement go to the same Bow Street extradition judge who so straightforwardly rejected the idea that a military commission conforms with the fair trial guarantees of the European Convention. On the isolation imposed by pre-trial SAMs he expressed extreme anxiety—'It is in relation to these that I find the greatest grounds for concern'—and in the case of one man, Abu Hamza, so disabled that he was likely if convicted to be imprisoned only briefly in ADX Florence before transfer to a prison hospital, the same judge found that 'but for that fact' such brutal isolation would violate Article 3, the prohibition against torture.

But these same brutal facts have been largely sidestepped by judges in the higher courts and by the government, who present reassurance in the shape of illusory legal protections for the prisoner once extradited the US: 'For a mature and sophisticated democracy that respects the rule of law, it would be unusual, to say the least, if one of its lawful and carefully prescribed methods of incarceration were to be condemned for giving rise to an automatic violation of Article 3.' The inclusion of the word 'automatic' is intended to describe the protection that litigation provides for a prisoner once in solitary confinement, but the prospects for any effective challenge in the US are nonexistent; there is no funding to support prisoner litigation and administrative obstacles prevent even the most determined of litigants from having his case heard within ten years. In any event, prisoners who go for years without speaking to anyone other than Federal Bureau of Prison officials have not been able to establish a claim under the Eighth Amendment to the constitution, which prohibits cruel and unusual punishment, since human contact has not been identified as a 'single identifiable human need such as warmth, food or exercise'. Extreme isolation, even for life, is not considered under the US constitution to be a denial of the 'minimal civilised measure of life's necessities'.

Strasbourg, Europe's court of last resort, has been criticised in the past for a lack of imagination, or at least of judicial understanding, when it comes to the impact of solitary confinement on prisoners, and of having 'too ready an acceptance of state interests'. On the one hand it has been reluctant to judge actual solitary confinement regimes as being in violation of the Convention, but yet has reminded itself of the irreducible nature of Article 3 in the context of fighting terrorism or crime:

> States face very real difficulties in protecting their populations from terrorist violence ... the Convention prohibits in absolute terms torture and inhuman or degrading treatment or punishment, irrespective of the conduct of the person concerned. The nature of the offence allegedly committed by the applicant is therefore irrelevant for the purposes of Article 3.

But it is precisely the 'nature of the offence' that will condemn the extraditees to conditions of imprisonment and sentences that are an inevitable consequence of the civilian trials that constitutionalists argue for, embedded as these practices have become within an entirely constitutional structure. Is indefinite military detention any worse a prospect?

One young American citizen, Syed Fahad Hashmi, who expected as his constitutional entitlement a speedy trial and humane conditions if imprisoned, was due to stand trial at the end of April 2010 in Manhattan. He had been held in the UK's Belmarsh prison before his extradition to the US in the same open conditions as all other prisoners, for an allegation that if tried in the UK would have merited at most a sentence of no more than two or three years. But after his extradition he was buried alive, in total isolation in a tiny cell, and never, for three years after arriving in his New York prison, saw the light of day. In those three years he experienced every coercive and unconstitutional practice at issue in the extraditions still outstanding.

His trial, under our Anglo-American adversarial process, promised fairness, a guarantee of equality of arms between prosecution and defendant. Yet Hashmi, under the disabilities that years of solitary confinement inevitably create, even for the strongest and the fittest, faced a prosecution based upon the evidence of a cooperating witness who pleaded guilty in the US to his own active engagement in terrorist activity in Pakistan involving explosives and, he claimed, the attempted murder of the country's president. The witness, having served the shortest of prison terms in the US, and having given evidence against others in a cluster of trials in a range of jurisdictions, claimed that Hashmi, a student in England, permitted him to leave a suitcase in his London flat in which there were combat clothes and lent him his phone on which he, the witness, telephoned a suspected terrorist in the UK. This was enough to secure Hashmi's extradition. For this, the cooperating witness now goes free and his victim, imprisoned in New York, was due to stand trial on charges of providing material support for terrorism before a jury surrounded by a political debate on the very propriety of the trial itself. Despite maintaining his innocence throughout, on the eve of his trial and faced with the prospect, if convicted, of a sentence of seventy years, he too capitulated and agreed instead to plead guilty.

Observations are easily made on the defects of one jurisdiction from the safety of another. The beam in our own national eye has involved indefinite detention without trial and complicity in torture perpetrated by others. We have in the UK been excused the responsibility of having to fight to end capital punishment in our own country or to participate in direct action to bring an end to the offshore illegality of Guantánamo. It is entirely by accident that we have come to see what remains unknown, we suspect, to most Americans. It leads us to believe that would be tragic if the constitutional battle today in the US to reclaim principles hammered out by Madison and Jefferson to protect not against the tyrant long ago overthrown, but against themselves for the future, did not find a way to question too other principles as centrally important and as deserving of constitutional protection; the building blocks of due process and humane treatment.

The granting of an interim freezing order for any extradition case by the European Court is exceptional and the length of time, now three years, that the Court has taken to wrestle with the acute legal problems thrown up by the practices of the United States in these cases is unprecedented. But whether or not Strasbourg constructs moral as well as legal barriers to which the US must pay heed if it continues to demand the presence on US soil of extraditees, Americans, simply by looking very near to home, should appreciate harsh truths in large part ignored to be as vital constitutionally as those other very public battles that many principled defenders of the rule of law in the US are now determinedly fighting.

May 2010

Postscript

It is difficult to record with precision the present as it turns continuously into history. The separate observations collected together in this book comment on a number of circumstances which appear, by August 2010, to have altered dramatically. Does the alteration, though, represent a truly radical shift, or something less?

This summer in Derry, for instance, the families of the thirteen individuals murdered on Bloody Sunday have had delivered to them, finally, the report of the Saville Inquiry. Their joy at the public statement of what, of course, had always been so—their relatives' innocence—was wonderful. This was a triumph of moral stamina; they had compelled the state, after more than half a lifetime, to carry out the investigation that had been its duty from the start. What had changed in the thirty-eight years in between was not, however, the discovery of new evidence that could establish, finally, who was innocent and who guilty, but the alteration of political convenience as to how the state chose to allocate criminality. After all, this most brazen of crimes carried out in broad daylight had been witnessed by thousands at the time.

On its heels, and in another shift of political pragmatism, the new coalition government, very soon after coming into office, announced a second inquiry, this time to investigate the complaints of complicity of British intelligence agencies in the torture of British citizens and British residents elsewhere in the world, now long and loudly voiced by the survivors.

Is it too grudging to see not only the proposed second inquiry, but the first too, as fitting too closely in the mould they were thought to be breaking? Saville's conclusions are that one platoon of the Parachute Regiment and one commander bear responsibility and that the chain of command above them could not have foreseen the events of the day. One of the few non-lawyers to have sat through the whole Saville Inquiry and to have read the whole of its lengthy report, Eamon McCann, has observed its startling omissions. The inquiry, in its exhaustive evidence, heard that in Derry the chief of police, Frank Lagan; the commander of the battalion garrisoned there, Peter Welsh; aide de camp to the head of the British Army Field Marshall Carver and Chief of Staff of the British Army David Ramsbotham (who delivered a warning to Carver minutes before as he entered a cabinet meeting) had all protested repeatedly in advance at the madness of bringing in the Paras to police a civil rights demonstration. The previous August, soldiers from the same regiment had shot dead eleven innocent civilians in a copybook operation in Ballymurphy, an incident into which the Saville Inquiry did not venture; nor did it consider the implications of the evidence of Ramsbotham and Welsh, that the orders to go in were coming from the top, i.e. from the cabinet in London. And there is no finding in the inquiry's report either that foresight existed or could have prevented the bloody events of the day, which even at the time were immediately recognised by Irish men and women as the actions not of a few rogue soldiers but as actions authorised at the highest level. In response, two days later the British Embassy in Dublin was burned down and there was a nationwide general strike across the Irish Republic, involving every trade union; airports, ports and pubs all closed. If so substantial an inquiry now could arrive at conclusions that allowed David Cameron to say to the House of Commons that the buck stops with the foot soldiers, has the British state in fact owned up to the whole truth? In age after age, societies look back and ask how it was that so many went along with what happened and with the consequences. Without knowing and accepting the truth in its entirety, how do we re-order the society in which we live? Nor is it possible to do so without an unqualified commitment to the principle fundamental to the rule of law: that it applies to all, without exception.

How does the precedent set by the Saville Inquiry inform us for so important an inquiry as the second, announced only this summer, into torture? This second inquiry has appointed as its chair a judge, Sir Peter Gibson, whose role for more than four years has been to provide statutory oversight of the Security and Intelligence Services whose very operations the inquiry must investigate. His view of the trustworthiness of their personnel is already on record. The government has given him, and his two panel members, the authority to set the inquiry's terms. There is nothing in David Cameron's announcement that guarantees that any of it will be heard in public; in contesting civil claims brought by the men who were tortured, the government has already fought (and recently failed) to create a secret court to hear those claims and, in the process, demolish 800 years of legal precedent; it is now instead attempting urgently to negotiate a settlement and thus avoid the further disclosure of documents to support (or contradict) the government's and the intelligence agencies' defence to the litigation. Were they or were they not complicit? And at what level? What emerges from the few documents so far reluctantly disclosed by the summer of 2010, after two years of litigation, is disturbingly familiar. Far from one or two maverick intelligence officers ignoring or exploiting the clear, terrible ill-treatment of their own countrymen before their eyes, in Bagram or in Guantánamo Bay, from the time of the first days of the men's capture in early 2002, the official email correspondence says it all. The chilling series of exchanges shows ministers communicating that they did not want the men back in their own country at any cost and that the most satisfactory solution for the UK was for all to be transported (entirely unlawfully) to Guantánamo Bay. But first a request from the very top: they should be held for a week (in unlawful conditions of extreme severity) so that they could be interrogated more conveniently by our own intelligence agents. And in response to anxieties on the part of foreign office officials expressed in emails passing back and forth that they were being complicit in unlawfully withholding from one man consular access (and with it the guarantee of his return to this country), the internal memoranda make it clear that the orders to do so were coming 'from No. 10'. It is with these clues that an inquiry to establish responsibility and criminality, which may well sit almost entirely in private, seems a most convenient template for the executive.

At every turn the undertow of political expediency drags back the advance by individuals towards certainty of their rightful entitlements in law. Today Cardinal O'Brien, the Catholic primate of Scotland, injects a moral commentary into the determined efforts of US senators to question British and Scottish politicians on the circumstances that surrounded the transfer to Libya of the dying al-Megrahi, convicted of the Lockerbie bombing. He questions the cruelty of an appetite for lifetime imprisonment which represents nothing more than an insatiable desire for vengeance. His words of moral authority coincide exactly with legal questions posed this summer to the United Kingdom by the European Court of Human Rights in relation to the cases of those men the UK has proposed to extradite to America for the past three and a half years. These questions strike at the heart of the same issue—the condoning of cruel and inhuman treatment. 'Is the 8th Amendment protection of the American Constitution', asks the Court, 'equivalent to the protection of Article 3 of the European Convention of Human Rights?' If it is not, then the way America treats its prisoners, and the extraordinary sentences to which it exposes them, may, from the perspective of the European Court, constitute prohibited punishment, tantamount to torture.

The catastrophe wreaked by British Petroleum on US shores has turned the minds of senators there to the very obvious fact that al-Megrahi's transfer coincided with urgent negotiations on access to Libya's oil by BP. But the larger unanswered question still hangs in the air: Have we been told what actually happened that led to the conviction of al-Megrahi, or was his conviction, too, a mockery of a construct built to fit the perceived political imperatives of the day? Many of the families of those who died when Pan Am 103 exploded over Lockerbie in 1988 have urged, for almost as long as the Bloody Sunday families, that there be a searching inquiry into what happened and not one focused instead on the decision, a proper one, and entirely customary in this country, to release a terminally ill person from prison.

Another dying man in a British prison years before, Giuseppe Conlon, wrongly convicted on the evidence of the same discredited scientists who provided the forensic case against al-Megrahi, was forced to wait for such a decision until the day of his death when the home secretary, fearful of a political backlash, agreed too late to his release on humanitarian grounds. But the desire for vengeance remained in the air. The family's undertaker in Belfast tells the story. The staff at Aldergrove Airport refused to handle his coffin; his body was flown back to England three times. A British Army officer, after Conlon's body was flown to Belfast a fourth time, informed the undertaker, 'It is on that plane but it is not coming off. The problem is the press have been notified and we can't be seen to be handling the body of an IRA man.'

When what alters is only the way society chooses to look, is it false optimism constantly to assert that there are rights, and that they are inalienable? In correspondence, arguing for the addition of a bill of rights to the US constitution in 1788, James Madison wrote 'experience proves the inefficacy on those occasions when its control is most needed. Repeated violations of these parchment barriers have been committed by overbearing majorities in every state.' Notwithstanding that, he endorsed such a bill because he believed it would at least 'counteract the impulses of interest and passion'. Thomas Jefferson replied from Paris that 'though it is not always efficacious under all circumstances, it is of great potency always and rarely inefficacious. A brace the more will often keep up the building which would have fallen, with that brace the less.'

August 2010